Exploring the
AMAZON

By Helen *and* Frank Schreider
With Photographs by the Authors
Foreword by Gilbert M. Grosvenor
Produced by the Special Publications Division, Robert L. Breeden, *Chief*
National Geographic Society, Washington, D. C.
Melvin M. Payne, *President*
Melville Bell Grosvenor, *Editor-in-Chief*
Frederick G. Vosburgh, *Editor*

EXPLORING THE AMAZON
By HELEN and FRANK SCHREIDER

Published by
THE NATIONAL GEOGRAPHIC SOCIETY
MELVIN M. PAYNE, *President*
MELVILLE BELL GROSVENOR,
    Editor-in-Chief
FREDERICK G. VOSBURGH, *Editor*
GILBERT M. GROSVENOR, *Executive
    Editor for this series*
ANDREW H. BROWN, *Consulting Editor*
DR. WOLFRAM U. DREWES, *Consultant
    Assistant Director, Department of Economic
    Affairs, Organization of American States*
DALE W. KIETZMAN, *Consultant
    Area Director, South America, Summer
    Institute of Linguistics*

Prepared by
THE SPECIAL PUBLICATIONS DIVISION
ROBERT L. BREEDEN, *Editor*
DONALD J. CRUMP, *Associate Editor*
LEON M. LARSON, *Manuscript Editor*
LINDA M. BRIDGE, *Research and Style*
Illustrations
BRYAN HODGSON, *Picture Editor*
JOSEPH A. TANEY, *Art Director*
JOSEPHINE B. BOLT, *Assistant Art Director*
RONALD M. FISHER, H. ROBERT MORRI-
    SON, GERALD S. SNYDER, *Picture Legends*
MARGERY G. DUNN, *Picture Legend Research*
PEGGY D. WINSTON, *Research Assistant*
JOHN D. GARST, JR., MONICA WOOD-
    BRIDGE, *Map Research and Production*
Production and Printing
ROBERT W. MESSER, *Production Manager*
ANN H. CROUCH, *Production Assistant*
JAMES R. WHITNEY, JOHN R. METCALFE,
    Engraving and Printing

WILLIAM L. ALLEN, CONSTANCE D. BROWN,
    SUZANNE J. JACOBSON, JOAN PERRY,
    SANDRA A. TURNER, *Staff Assistants*
JOLENE MCCOY, *Index*

*Digging savagely at the swirling water with a hand-
hewn paddle, Frank Schreider strains to free the authors'
balsa-wood raft from the clutches of a whirlpool on the
Ene River in Peru, some 500 miles below the source of
the Amazon. Overleaf: Two name changes later, as the
Ucayali, the growing stream meanders past oxbow lakes
created as it cuts across loops of its course. Page 1 and
book binding: Triangular sail billowing in the breeze, a
Brazilian riverboat plies the lower reaches of the Amazon.*

HELEN AND FRANK SCHREIDER, RIGHT AND PAGES 2-3;
PAGE 1: LOREN MCINTYRE

Foreword

WITH A HANDSHAKE, we sealed our wager. I felt certain that Helen and Frank Schreider could not travel in just four weeks from the source of the Amazon River, high in the Andes, to Pucallpa, Peru—the first major city along the river. Reaching Pucallpa safely seemed especially important to us at the time. We thought that by then the most dangerous leg of the entire journey would be behind them—the rapids of the Apurímac, headwater of the Amazon.

Perhaps I had a slight advantage when I made the wager, for I could vividly recall the stories that my grandfather, Gilbert H. Grosvenor, had told me about Teddy Roosevelt's experiences in the Amazon Basin. One summer evening in 1914, grandfather—then President and Editor of the National Geographic—introduced T. R. to an audience of Society members. The former President had returned that very day to Washington from a trip down a tributary of the Amazon—Brazil's Rio da Duvida, the River of Doubt. In a voice weakened by illness and exhaustion, the old Rough Rider told of the price exacted from his party of explorers by the jungle's green hell, of rapids and piranhas, of Indians and giant insects, of snakes and jungle madness.

While I was sure the Schreiders would survive their ordeal on the treacherous Amazon, I knew they would face formidable obstacles.

A year later I collected my wager, the best dinner in town—at the Schreiders' home. They barely had missed their four-week goal. After properly toasting the mighty Amazon, Frank announced: "It's true Helen and I lost our race to Pucallpa. Perhaps if we had hurried, we also would have lost our lives as have so many explorers before us. We are proud to be the first couple to journey the Amazon from its source to its mouth."

Then came the surprise: "Gil, we are convinced we can firmly establish that the Amazon—not the Nile—is the world's longest river."

He was spoiling for another wager, but I demurred, warning him, "You'll have a tough time proving it!" But Frank accepted the challenge as just one more the Amazon had to offer.

As I suspected, a dispute did arise. It centers on the Pará River—the Schreiders' route south of Marajó Island to the Atlantic. In their calculations Helen and Frank, like many geographers, considered the Pará as part of the Amazon's mouth and arrived at a total distance of 4,195 miles, at least 50 more than the length of the Nile. But some experts argue that the Pará is part of another river system. Incredible as it may seem, no international geographic body exists today with the authority to review and rule on such issues.

So, as this book goes to press, I'm pleased to report that officers of your Society have determined to study the question and, we hope, bring agreement on the lengths of the world's major rivers.

Since the day of the conquistadors, the Amazon has lured explorers and adventurers. Many have left records of their experiences, but few accounts are so filled with the excitement of discovery as *Exploring the Amazon,* a stirring tribute to the courage of its authors.

GILBERT M. GROSVENOR

At a floating market in Manaus, Brazil, waterborne vendors
peddle produce fresh from the jungle that hems the city.

The Amazon and Its Vast Basin: A River

NDER OTHER CIRCUMSTANCES I might have sensed the portent of our friend's question. But in the oak-paneled lounge of Lima's Hotel Bolívar, with pisco sours frosty on the table before us, the warning escaped me. The Amazon was still far away, and I was too elated by our effortless passage through Peruvian customs with 22 cases of photographic equipment, camping gear, and concentrated food, plus a big German shepherd named Balthazar.

"Do you know what Apurímac means?" our Peruvian friend repeated.

I confessed that at the moment I was more concerned with finding the headwaters of the Apurímac River—the Amazon's source tributary—than I was with the meaning of its name.

"Well, you really should be concerned, you know, if you're planning to run it. More than one explorer has drowned in it. The Incas called the river Apurímac—Great Speaker—because of the roar of its rapids."

My wife Helen, sitting across from me, glanced down at her pisco, the brown bitters floating like flotsam on the frothy pale grape brandy and lime juice. I knew what she was thinking. Rapids had been her special fear ever since she had seen a companion's kayak break up on the rocks of a fast Alaskan river.

On our first trip to Peru 13 years earlier we had stopped on a bridge spanning the Apurímac near Cuzco and looked down on the green water laced with white, and I had shown Helen on a map how the Apurímac became the Ene and the Ene became the Tambo and the Tambo became the Ucayali and the Ucayali became the Amazon—that mighty brown flood that drains the largest jungle in the world. She had known then that someday we would travel this river of legend and mystery and controversy. Now the time had come, and I wondered: How much of what we had read and heard of the Amazon really was true, how much was pure fiction, how much fanciful exaggeration?

The Amazon has lent itself to exaggeration since the day the Spaniard Francisco de Orellana sailed onto it in 1542. His story of battling warrior women, so similar to the Amazons of Greek myth, gave the river the name by which we know her today. In Orellana's time the conquistadors called her Mar Dulce, Freshwater Sea. Río de Marañas, River of Entanglements, others called her— those who survived her hazards. Old maps record still more names—Río

Clinging lianas climb past a Yagua Indian hunter armed with a blowgun—a primitive but deadly weapon. His jungle-choked world, the Amazon Basin, remains largely uninhabited, mostly unexplored, and one of earth's last strongholds of the unknown.

# of Legend, a Land of Mystery

Cordillera Huayhuash peaks rise above Lake Lauricocha, Peru, once considered the Amazon's source.

Geographers recently established the true source—a spring at the head of Peru's Apurímac River.

Wearing tightly woven bark cloth as protection against a drenching rain, a Chacobo Indian paddles through a flooded forest in Bolivia's northeastern province of Beni. The Amazon drains great areas of six nations: Brazil, Peru, Ecuador, Colombia, Venezuela, and Bolivia. Below, a Campa Indian stalks fish beside the Apurímac River, a Peruvian tributary of the Amazon. The setting sun gilds his bow and arrow.

Grande, Solimões, Orellana — names as varied as the legends her jungle spawns.

Even today tales of white Indians, lost cities, lodes of pure gold, and snakes 60 feet long continue to filter from her forests to titillate the imagination.

And yet her legends pale beside the truth, for the Amazon is more than a river. Her questing arms, like veins in a green leaf carpeting half a continent, reach into six countries, etching their courses through Venezuela, Colombia, Ecuador, Peru, Bolivia, and Brazil. From snowy Andean peaks to misty jungle, the Amazon gathers her strength. Rising within 120 miles of the Pacific she heads north, then east, paralleling the Equator, crossing South America, collecting melting snow, mountain springs, jungle dew, and rain until at the Atlantic she spills from her mouth one-fifth of all the fresh water discharged by rivers into all the seas of all the world.

Her volume of flow exceeds that of the Mississippi 11 times over. Her navigable waterways total an estimated 50,000 miles. Of her 1,100 major tributaries 10 are longer than the Rhine. An ocean-going freighter can sail 2,300 miles up the Amazon and in a few places find water beneath its keel deep enough to cover a 10-story building. In the 599 miles from its source to Atalaya the river drops 16,000 feet, a phenomenal average of 26.5 feet per mile. From Atalaya to the Atlantic it falls only 700 feet, roughly a quarter-inch per mile.

The Amazon Basin, the area nourished by the mighty river and its tributaries, covers 2.3 million square miles — a region two-thirds the size of the 50 United States. The basin's streams support some 2,000 species of fish, compared with only 250 for the Mississippi.

Among the untold thousands of species of insects that populate the Amazon's forests are the world's largest ant, *Dinoponera gigantea*, which grows to 1.4 inches in length, and one of the world's biggest beetles, the 6-inch-plus *Titanus giganteus*. The basin also harbors the world's longest snake, the giant anaconda, stretching as long as 38 feet, and the world's biggest rodent, the capybara, measuring up to 4 feet from head to tail.

Four centuries of explorers and exploiters, soldiers, slavers, and scientists have sought to probe her secrets and tap her wealth. During the great rubber boom — the quarter-century from 1890 to 1915 when the Amazon forest was the only source of the white latex that the world rides on today — villages grew into cities almost overnight. Iquitos in Peru and Manaus and Belém in Brazil throbbed with an opulence that rivaled the golden grandeur of the Incas. And almost as quickly they went back to sleep again, leaving a legacy of legends to feed the aspirations of a new generation of adventurers.

Today prospectors range the Amazonian jungles in helicopters and light planes in search of diamonds, gold, and oil. Instead of bringing logs to the sawmills, lumbermen bring sawmills to the logs. The six countries whose watersheds feed the Amazon are beginning to develop her hidden, long-neglected riches. Gradually the world is learning more about the geography of this fantastic river. Only a few years ago even its source was in question.

Oddly enough, the search for the source of the Amazon never excited the world's imagination as did the search for the source of the Nile. The Amazon has never had its Herodotus or Ptolemy, its Burton, Speke, Baker, or Livingstone, men who long pondered the origin of Africa's longest river. Even Francisco de Orellana, the first European to lead an *(Continued on page 18)*

Molten lava and ash spew from the fiery crater (opposite) of Ecuador's 17,159-foot Sangay Volcano — one stage of the mountain-building that launched the upthrust of the Andes some 70 million years ago and continues to shape them today. Heavy rainfall along the mountains' eastern slopes nurtures highland tributaries of the Amazon. Seen from 40 miles away (above), Sangay emerges from the clouds. Below, snow clings to the very edge of the smoking crater.

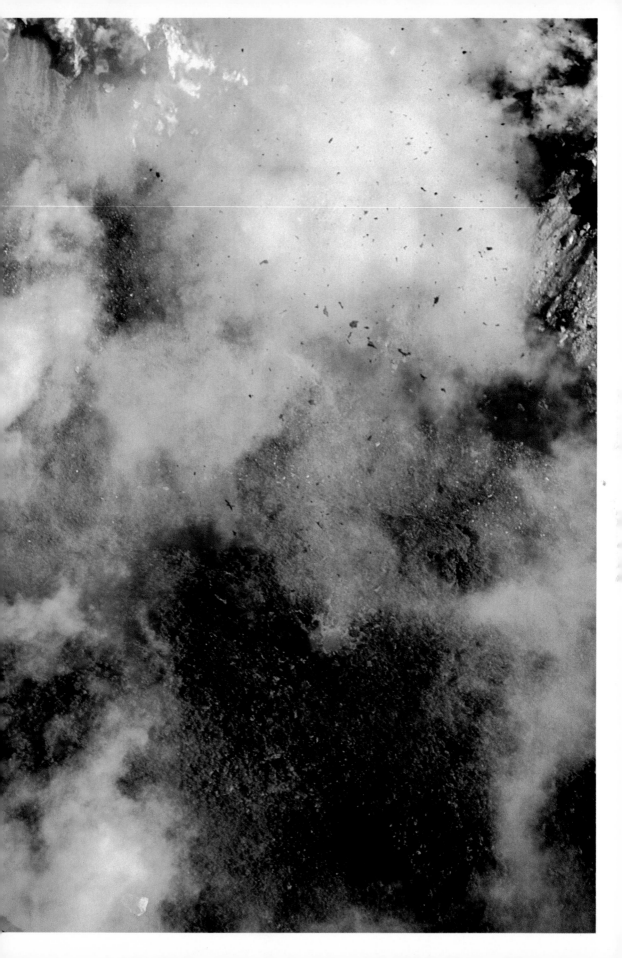

Mountains rim Izcuchaca, a Peruvian village little touched by time. A Spanish-colonial bridge spans the Mantaro River, a tributary of the Apurímac. Many Andean highlanders—like the women of Chincheros (below)—dress in centuries-old costumes. They weave their cloth of cotton and of wool from llamas or alpacas. Extinction threatens another source of wool, the vicuña. A newborn fawn (bottom) soaks up sun at a Peruvian ranch; conservationists hope to domesticate, and thus save, the species.

HELEN AND FRANK SCHREIDER (ABOVE) AND LOREN McINTYRE (RIGHT)

NATIONAL GEOGRAPHIC PHOTOGRAPHER GEORGE F. MOBLEY

Curl-crested toucans scream at 19th-century naturalist Henry Walter Bates as he retrieves a wounded member of the flock (opposite). During his 11-year pioneering study of animal life in the Amazon Basin, Bates collected specimens of more than 14,500 species, 8,000 of them new to science. On a 1588 Dutch map of South America, Jodocus Hondius included an inset (below) showing Indians brewing and drinking a root beverage. The German cartographer Thedor de Bry imagined a serpentine course for the Amazon River in a work completed four years later (bottom).

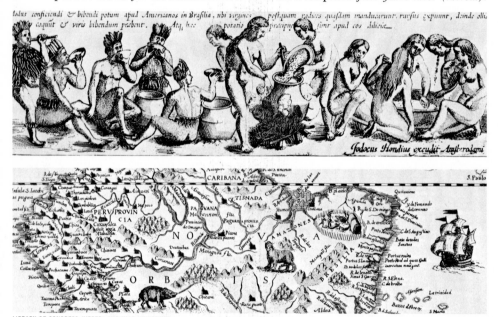

expedition down the Amazon, did so by accident, starting on a relatively minor tributary in Ecuador. And the American explorer U. S. Navy Lt. William Lewis Herndon traveled the Huallaga and the Marañón in the belief that the latter was the source tributary of the Amazon because of its great volume of flow.

Today, however, by internationally accepted definition the source of a river is considered to be the point where its longest tributary rises. In 1953 the French explorer Michel Perrin pointed out that the Ucayali and its extension the Apurímac, which springs from Mount Huagra some 130 miles south of Cuzco, is the longest tributary. Most authorities, including the National Geographic Society, now accept Mount Huagra as the Amazon's source, but its length has never been accurately established.

Since man first measured the world's great rivers, the Nile has ranked as the longest, with the Amazon running second. Perrin believed that the Amazon was considerably longer than had been credited, and attempted to prove it by traveling from Mount Huagra to the Atlantic. When his expedition ended tragically with the death of his companion in the rapids of the Apurímac, the faint ripples generated by his efforts subsided. (Continued on page 27)

Fantastic forms and colors emerge among myriad species of Amazonian insects. The slant-faced grasshopper, Omura congrua *(right), common to most of the region, peers through jewel-like eyes set on the sides of its conical head. A 1^1/$_4$-inch-long prionid beetle (left), probably* Pyrodes sp., *a wood borer, thrives in dead tree branches. The iridescent giant,* Morpho didius, *below, one of some 1,800 species of butterflies in the Amazon Basin, often attains a wingspread of 7 inches.*

Shield with sharp-tipped points (above) disguises a buffalo treehopper, Ceresa *sp., shown eight times its natural size. Many Amazonian members of this common family of sapsuckers, the Membracidae, have developed bizarre shapes resembling thorny parts of plants they frequent.*

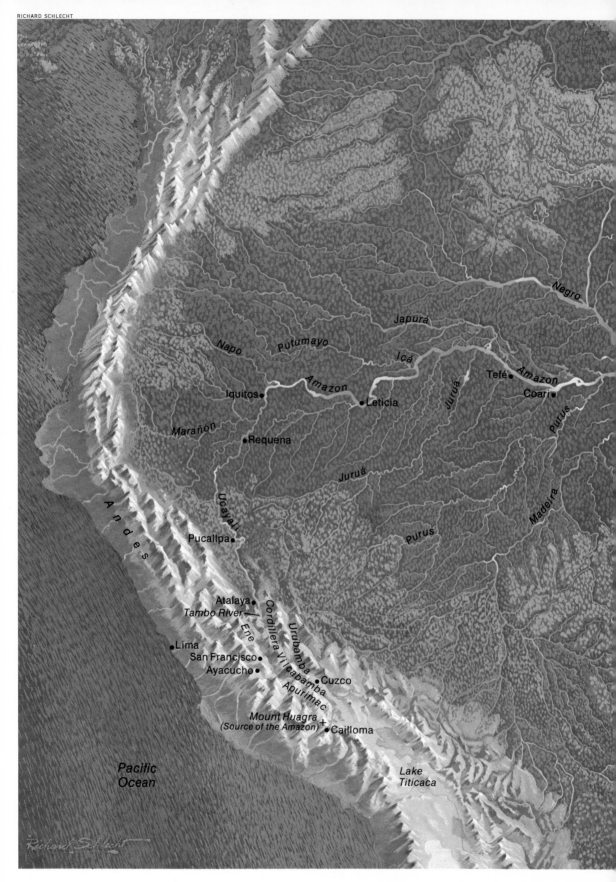

Negro

Japurá

Napo   Putumayo

Içá

Tefé Amazon

Amazon

Coari

Iquitos

Leticia

Juruá

Marañón

Purus

Requena

Juruá

Ucayali

Purus

Madeira

Pucallpa

Andes

Atalaya
Tambo River

Cordillera Vilcabamba

Lima
San Francisco
Ayacucho

Ene

Urubamba

Cuzco

Apurímac

Mount Huagra
(Source of the Amazon)
Cailloma

Pacific
Ocean

Lake
Titicaca

Richard Schlecht

Born high in the Andes, the Amazon surges toward the Atlantic, growing with every mile. More than

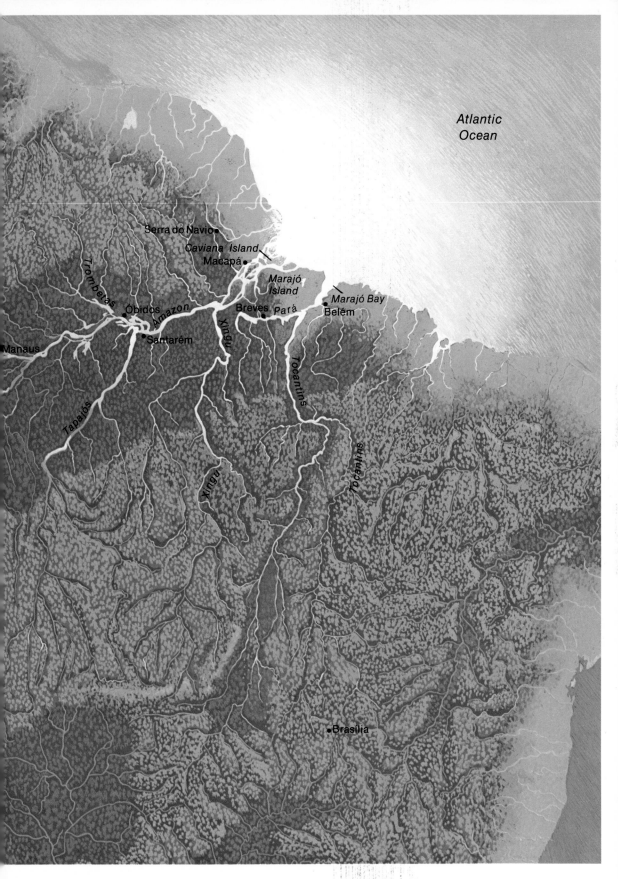

Atlantic
Ocean

Serra do Navio
Caviana Island
Macapá
Marajó
Island
Trombetas
Óbidos   Amazon   Breves   Pará   Marajó Bay
                                              Belém
Manaus   Santarém
                                    Xingu
                                              Tocantins
Tapajós

Xingu   Tocantins

Brasília

a thousand major tributaries drain the 2.3-million-square-mile basin of the world's mightiest river.

23

Woman of La Oroya, Peru, carries her child and laundry up from the Mantaro River (opposite). On the other bank, a smelter processes Peru's leading mineral export, copper, as well as other metals. A hydroelectric dam under construction nearby (below left) will harness the power of the river. Increasing industrialization of the upper Amazon Basin hardly affects most highlanders; village women lug heavy adobes (below right) to build a school at Ataura, Peru. Buses (bottom) travel an expanding network of roads, linking towns on Amazon headwaters with the Pacific coast.

Six-month-old Andean condor balances on the glove of ornithologist Jerry McGahan in Colombia. When grown, the fledgling may attain a wingspread of 10 feet. McGahan and his wife study the birds with National Science Foundation and National Geographic Society support. Llamas (below), Andean beasts of burden first domesticated 2,500 years ago, wear wool strands — marks of ownership — in their ears.

Perrin was not the first to raise such a question. In 1949 O. R. Walkey, a British missionary on the Amazon for many years and fellow of the Royal Geographical Society, measured the river from near its true source, using the best maps available at the time, and arrived at a figure of 4,050 statute miles, or some 80 miles longer than the then-accepted length of the Nile.

Supporters of the Nile as the longest river rose in arms, questioning the accuracy of Mr. Walkey's figures, and geographers adopted a compromise length of 3,912 miles for the Amazon. Later, E. J. Devroey, administrator of the Hydrographic Committee of the Belgian Congo, remeasured the Nile, using more-detailed maps, many of them on a scale of 1:200,000, or approximately 3 miles to the inch. His figure of 4,145 miles for the Nile remained unchallenged until the creation of Lake Nasser. Backing up from the Aswan High Dam, the lake is eliminating miles of meanders, thus reducing the length of the Nile.

Helen and I began to suspect that the Amazon might be even longer than Walkey's computations had indicated. And later as we traveled the river, our suspicions grew with each passing day. Although *(Continued on page 36)*

Visitors enter the mouth (opposite) of the Cueva de las Lechuzas—Cave of the Owls—near Tingo María, Peru. Natives of the region mistook for owls the hundreds of hawk-size oilbirds the cave shelters (below). A sonarlike sense enables the nocturnal creatures to navigate among the grotesque limestone formations.

Host of pierid butterflies — a common sight throughout much of Amazonia — flecks the breeze with gold

as Indian children float along the cloud-dappled Vaupés River, a Colombian tributary of the Rio Negro.

Varied faces of the Amazon Basin: Mission-school students splash in the Paca River (opposite), a Colombian tributary of the Rio Negro. Below, a smiling youngster wears the red beret of her kindergarten in Belém, Brazil. A Quechua miner works a silver vein near Cailloma, Peru. Tribal markings line the face of a Campa Indian girl. Bamboo plugs, incised with geometric designs, extend downward from the ears of an Achual Indian. Toucan-feather headdress, face paint, and bound braids complete his finery.

LOREN McINTYRE (OPPOSITE, UPPER AND LOWER LEFT)
AND HELEN AND FRANK SCHREIDER

Always changing, the Amazon yet remains the same amid the cycles of youth and age, wealth and want along its banks. Below, a family bathes in silt-laden water at Belén, a floating suburb of Iquitos, Peru. An old man looks onto a street of Manaus, Brazil (lower opposite), from his tenement in a decaying mansion that recalls an era of affluent rubber barons. Grizzled caretaker (right) tends a cemetery at Santarém, Brazil.

HELEN AND FRANK SCHREIDER (OPPOSITE) AND LOREN McINTYRE

we were able to gauge our own speed and that of the current, we seldom attained the daily mileage that our charts indicated we should. From such seeds we began our studies. But how does one go about measuring a river when much of it never has been mapped accurately?

We took the problem to Dr. Wolfram U. Drewes of the Organization of American States, a geographer and old friend with many years of experience in the little-known Peruvian section of the Amazon. Through him we learned that much of the region in question only recently had been mapped at large scale to evaluate natural resources. In addition, aerial photographs were available of areas not yet compiled into maps.

José Lizarraga Reyes, director of Peru's National Office for the Evaluation of Natural Resources, provided the maps and photographic mosaics. Comdr. Nelson A. Xavier, assistant naval attaché at the Brazilian Embassy in Washington, D. C., and Comdr. Alvaro Paim Filho, chief of Brazil's Hydrographic Office in Rio de Janeiro, supplied navigational charts on a larger scale than anything heretofore used to measure the Amazon. Col. E. C. Bruce, director of the Inter-American Geodetic Survey, members of the British Admiralty, and officials of Booth Steamship Company, Ltd. — which has maintained service on the Amazon for more than half a century — also lent their support to the project.

When we put all these charts and photographs together, we had the most detailed map of the Amazon ever assembled; from end to end it stretched almost 200 feet. Measuring it was a painstaking but exciting task. Only near the end did we encounter a serious difficulty: Should we consider the Pará River — our southerly route around Marajó Island — as part of the mouth of the Amazon or as a separate river system? This became a crucial distinction because the Pará course is 188 miles longer than the northern channel, the most direct route to the Atlantic Ocean.

Experts we consulted disagreed widely. Hydrologists tend to consider the Pará as part of a separate drainage system because of the minimal exchange of water between it and the Amazon. Geologists and geographers, we found, generally take another view. For example, the highly respected *Atlas do Brasil,* published by the Conselho Nacional de Geografia, states that "...the Pará River must be considered part of the mouth of the Amazon." Also, many countries — Brazil among them — normally measure delta channels via the most favorable navigation route for the largest ships using the system.

By its northern channel the Amazon measures 4,007 miles, according to our calculations. But measuring via the Pará,* the route most ships use, the world's mightiest river would also become the world's longest, stretching to 4,195 miles — 50 miles longer than the Nile.

As *Exploring the Amazon* goes to press, officers of the Society have undertaken a definitive study of the problem, bringing together leading authorities in the field to define the criteria for measuring rivers and to establish an officially accepted figure for the length of the Amazon.

This was the river of legend — of riddles — we had chosen to challenge. As we jetted toward Cuzco, our base for the journey to the headwaters of the Apurímac, we could not help wondering what the Great Speaker would tell us.

*Measurements of the Amazon used in subsequent chapters of this book are based on the route the authors followed, using this commonly traveled shipping channel.

Blazing lights illumine an office building under construction in Belém, Brazil. Ships generally enter the Amazon via this gateway port to avoid island-choked channels and treacherous tides to the north. A modern city of 625,000, Belém throbs with commerce and industry, mirroring dreams of those who seek to tap the Amazon Basin's wealth.

To the Source: A Mountain Spring That

CHAPTER TWO

REMENDOUS LUNG CAPACITY and superb conditioning prepared Inca couriers to run in relays from garrisons along the Pacific coast to Cuzco, their imperial capital high in the Andes, in three days. Spanning the same distance via jet from coastal Lima, Helen and I soon found that our 20-minute flight had left us ill equipped to cope with the thin, chill air of Cuzco's 11,150-foot elevation. However, any concern we might have had for Balty's adjustment to the abrupt change in altitude was quickly dispelled as he bounded from his crate, playfully — and permanently — scattering the porters who had come to help us with our baggage.

"Well," Helen puffed as we staggered to the taxi with our gear, "this should help put us in shape for the climb to the Apurímac's headwaters." Something would have to. Overnight we had passed from midsummer in Washington, D. C., to midwinter in Peru. Our contour maps defined the Apurímac as far upstream as the village of Cailloma, some 225 road miles south of Cuzco. But there the river divides into a web of waterways near 17,188-foot-high Mount Huagra.

By the time we had climbed the stairs to our second-floor room in the Hotel Cuzco, we had decided to condition ourselves on the city's hilly streets before heading any higher.

For us Cuzco — at the headwaters of the Huantanay River, itself a tributary of the Amazon — was familiar territory, a fascinating way-stop on a journey by amphibious jeep from Alaska to Tierra del Fuego 13 years earlier. In those days our semifluency in Spanish and adjustment to altitude had developed gradually as we drove south. What better place to reacquire both than this city of living history, where, with a little imagination, one can peel back the crust of the present and expose visions of the past glory of the Inca Empire, a glory built from "the sweat of the sun and the tears of the moon."

So the Incas called gold and silver. But to them the precious metals had little value except to honor the sun god and his direct descendant, the Inca, or Emperor. Extracted from rich, widely scattered mines, "sweat and tears" had rained on Cuzco for 300 years by the time the conquistadors, captained by Francisco Pizarro, landed on the Peruvian coast in 1532.

On two earlier voyages, Pizarro had heard tales of palaces sheathed in gold and temples lined with it. Near the Temple of the Sun in Cuzco, Inca artisans

Bent under his burden, a Quechua Indian trudges to market in Cuzco, Peru, past a wall constructed by Inca stonemasons in the 15th century. The Andean city served as a jumping-off point for Helen and Frank Schreider's climb to the Amazon's source.

Spawns a Mighty River Sea

Cuzco fans outward from the Plaza de Armas, heart of the city since its days of glory as the seat of a sprawling Inca Empire. Gold-hungry Spanish conquistadors razed much of the capital; later a new city rose, parts of it on pre-Columbian foundations. Builders used stones from Inca ruins to shape the steps of the Church of Belén (below left), where a Quechua woman spins alpaca wool. Green dye stains her hands. She may knit the yarn into chullos, *winter caps popular with tourists (bottom).*

had planted, as the contemporary historian Pedro de Cieza de León related, "...a garden in which the earth was lumps of fine gold ... with stalks of corn that were of gold—stalk, leaves, and ears.... so well planted that no matter how hard the wind blew it could not uproot them. Aside from this, there were more than twenty sheep of gold with their lambs, and the shepherds who guarded them, with their slings and staffs, all of this metal."

Pizarro and his small army—106 infantry and 62 cavalry—found the highly centralized Inca regime weakened by internal strife. In one boldly treacherous massacre lasting less than an hour, they virtually demolished it, capturing the Inca Atahuallpa. Bargaining for his freedom, Atahuallpa ordered his subjects to fill a room 17 feet wide and 22 feet long with gold to a 9-foot depth, plus a smaller room twice filled with silver—a ransom worth millions of dollars. But the bargain was in vain. Pizarro ordered the Inca ruler to trial on a series of trumped-up charges and executed him.

Thus began the deflowering of the Inca Empire. The conquistadors saw the sweat and tears as so many congealed ingots. They ripped the gold plate from the walls and forced the Inca craftsmen to destroy their own creations, melting down the suns and moons, shepherds and llamas, fountains and cornfields into easily transportable bars.

The gold and silver gone, the Spaniards quarried the temples, palaces, and fortresses, using the exquisitely worked stones to build churches and residences on Inca foundations. Today the curved wall of the Temple of the Sun supports the Church of Santo Domingo, and the Street of the Twelve-Cornered Stone borders the archbishop's house. Denuded of its towers, the fortress of Sacsahuamán stands its lonely vigil on Cuzco's outskirts. But when the sun slips behind the encircling hills and the city's lights sprinkle the golden afterglow with silver, Cuzco's ancient stones seem to cry out from the past, "See us for what we were, not for what we have become."

What Cuzco was has made it what it is—a leading attraction in South America for a kind of modern conquistador, the tourist. Singly or in groups—cameras, gadget bags, and tripods clanking like armor—vacationists fan out across the city with the relentless perseverance of an army on the attack, trying on alpaca caps or buying brass llamas for charm bracelets, or occasionally, when the church deems it surplus, an old religious painting of the once-renowned Cuzqueña school. Except for the revenue—industry-poor Cuzco would die without it—the thousand or so tourists the city can accommodate at any one time leave little impress.

Cuzco has always been an "international" city; at the height of Inca grandeur it housed 15,000 temporary residents—hostages, officials, couriers, and nobles from every part of the empire. Cieza de León tells us that each of the scores of tribes represented could be identified by its distinctive costume and headdress. Not one of them resembled the feathered, bare-chested, moccasined fugitive from a cigar store that stands in the Plaza de Armas, a 1920's product of an American sculptor who never saw Cuzco.

Had that sculptor visited Cuzco he might have formed a better idea of life during Inca times, different in detail, perhaps, but similar in spirit. On feast days of the important saints, when nearby towns spill their numbers into Cuzco, the people of Sicuani in their white straw hats and gay shawls and the

Morning sunlight sweeps across the terraces and white-granite ruins of Machu Picchu, an Inca stronghold the Spanish never found. From the citadel sheer cliffs plunge 2,000 feet; at their base the Urubamba River rushes to swell the Amazon. American explorer Hiram Bingham discovered the jungle-choked eyrie in 1911. The following year—heading an expedition sponsored jointly by Yale University and the National Geographic Society—Bingham returned to Peru to begin clearing the site.

Franciscan friar strides from La Compañia (background) toward the entrance to the Cathedral of Cuzco. Arriving with the conquistadors, Roman Catholic missionaries soon established the church as a powerful influence in the Andes. To cast the cathedral monstrance (below left), artisans melted 50 pounds of Inca gold, then encrusted it with more than a thousand jewels. Virgin and Child dominate a section of the baroque base of the Church of San Blas pulpit, carved out of cedar by an unknown Indian craftsman. At Chincheros, near Cuzco, villagers attend Mass (bottom).

villagers from Chincheros in their red-trimmed black ponchos and doughnut-shaped headgear gather in groups not unlike those the Inca saw when he surveyed his subjects on the noon of the summer solstice. Today life-size images of saints, bedecked with jewels and fine fabrics, are paraded on platforms through the streets; so too was the Inca carried through the throngs.

As the direct descendant of the sun the Inca decreed what a man could wear, when he could marry, where he could live, and how he could work. He took a third of the peasants' produce for himself and the priesthood, stored a third for protection against drought, and left a third for the people. Coca, the "divine plant" from which cocaine is extracted, he reserved for himself and his nobles and possibly for the *chasquis,* the couriers who maintained a far-reaching inter-urban communications system still unequaled in many parts of Peru. In return for all this, the Inca's control of grazing lands and llama herds assured a plentiful supply of wool as well as meat for the people of the empire. His well-stocked granaries and superb accounting system that kept track of every resource in the empire eased the effects of temporary shortages. His swift justice all but eliminated crime.

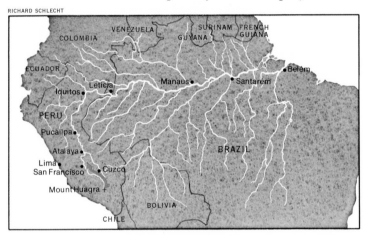

RICHARD SCHLECHT

From Cuzco the Schreiders travel to the source of the Amazon, then follow its winding course toward San Francisco.

Want was unknown. But so was individualism. More than horses, gunpowder, and steel, this lack of individualism—the inability of the people to think and plan for themselves—enabled Pizarro and his small army to subjugate the Inca Empire so effectively. That Conquest altered forever the ways of the highland Indian. Without the controls that had guaranteed him food and wool, that had prohibited him coca, he was lost. Life became the passive plea for survival that it often is today. Scratching with wooden tools in the poor rocky soil, the Indian struggles to keep food in his stomach and clothes on his back, and failing these stuffs his cheek with a cud of coca leaf to dim the pangs of hunger and cold. He finds release in the meadlike *chicha* and the pleasures of a feast day or marriage party when flutes, drums, and harps strike the haunting harmony of a *huyno*—a tune of the highlands—and the plodding step becomes a gay mimicry of a glorious past.

But all this is changing. The Indian is discovering a placebo more potent than coca. Far more rapidly than we could have predicted 13 years earlier, schools have come to the highlands. The coca addict's blackened teeth and bleary eyes, so universal on our first visit, today are giving way to the flashing smile and alert glance of Peru's youth.

Peru's youth descended on Cuzco en masse a few days after we arrived. On a week-long vacation from schools all over the country, they milled by the thousand through the alleylike streets. Leather jackets and Levis, tight toreador pants and turtleneck sweaters all but overwhelmed the shawls and ponchos in the plazas. When "rock" replaced the huyno in the record shop beneath our window, we retreated to the mountain sanctuary of Machu Picchu, but we found the "lost city of the Incas" anything but a sanctuary. Special tour trains had been added to handle the horde of holiday visitors. The small hotel, with rooms for only 26 people, frenetically served some 400 at lunch. Picnickers perched on the Inca sundial; in the Temple of the Three Windows, Beatlelike music twanged from hand-carried transistor radios; the paralyzing patter of guides droned across the semicircular Temple of the Chosen Women. From ten in the morning when the first tour train arrived until four in the afternoon when the last one left, Machu Picchu cringed under an onslaught it had never known during the years the conquistadors overran the country.

Regardless of all the tourist activity, for us Machu Picchu remains a dead city by day. It lives only at dawn and at sunset or under a full moon hanging low in the sky when dim, shadowy light softly sheens the polished stones and the wind sighs through a silence as deep as the void in Machu Picchu's history.

Who built this eyrie in the clouds 2,000 feet above the Urubamba River? Who lived here? Why was it abandoned, perhaps even before Pizarro launched his conquest? Archeologists have tried to answer these questions since 1911, when the American explorer Hiram Bingham stumbled on its ruins in his search for Vilcabamba, the last stronghold of the Incas.

Spanish literature, rich in detail about other Inca cities and cultures, makes no mention of Machu Picchu; and the Incas, advanced in astronomy, medicine, architecture, accounting, and social structure, never developed a written language. Machu Picchu probably will remain shrouded in mystery. Perhaps this is as it should be. In an age when science is weaving many diverse threads into a whole tapestry, we still need some place to unleash the shadowy ghosts of conjecture, to marvel at the daily miracle of a sunrise and the majesty of the moon. Machu Picchu is such a place.

The feeling lingered even back in Cuzco as we prepared for the journey to the source of the Amazon. Yawning sleepily in the predawn pink of a clear Andean morning, we checked our gear. Mountain tent. Down sleeping bags. Rucksacks. Hiking boots. Cameras, compass, altimeter, and maps. Ten days' ration of dehydrated food. With the help of Benigno, our driver, we loaded each item into his waiting sedan.

The route we followed toward Cailloma, the village closest to the source of the Apurímac, traced one of the lesser Inca roads. Llama trains carrying charcoal and firewood from remote wooded valleys kicked little puffs of dust from the washboard dirt track. The thin wail of a *quena*, the Quechua flute, drifted across the altiplano, or highland plateau, as some shepherd greeted the dawn. But most Andean people rise late, waiting until the sun creeps onto the valley floors to drive the frost from the winter-sere fields. It was midmorning before the smoke of cooking fires wreathed the grass-roofed adobe houses and life stirred in the streets of the villages along the way. A woman, bulky with child and still bundled in her llama-wool shawl, shook the sleep from her thick black braids and hung a white flag from her door, signaling that her chicha—brewed two days before—had aged enough to sell. From another door fluttered a wisp of twigs: Coca leaves had arrived from the lower valleys. A basket advertised freshly baked bread; a red flag, newly butchered llama or pig.

For a while we followed the green-fringed blue *(Continued on page 52)*

Patchwork croplands of an altiplano — a highland plateau — spread toward the lofty peaks of the Cordillera de Vilcanota. Working in a field, a Quechua woman (below) winnows barley with a wooden pitchfork. Antiquated farming methods, little changed since Inca times, help to foster a cycle of poverty that reduces many Andean Indians to impassive resignation. But growing governmental education programs today offer children like the young harvester (bottom) hope for a brighter future.

Journey to the source: Helen and an Indian mine worker-porter struggle past an ice cave as guide Jorge Palomino and Balthazar, the Schreiders' German shepherd, break trail up a snow-covered ridge. The authors hiked 19 miles round trip to the tiny year-round spring that trickles through the tundralike sod of Mount Huagra at an altitude of 17,000 feet. The spring forms a stream Indians call the Huaraco; as the Amazon, some 4,000 miles and 7 name-changes later, it flows into the Atlantic. At right, Balty quenches his thirst at the start of the world's mightiest river. Tracing the course downstream, the Schreiders pitched their tent (below) on a point where the Callomane (foreground) joins the Apurímac.

of the Vilcanota River; then we climbed from the valley and headed southwest toward Yauri, a village near the Apurímac en route to Cailloma. The road sliced between the brown stone walls of an Inca fort guarding the defile. Beneath the walls a farmer was whipping his span of five mules in circles, their hoofs flailing the husks from barley. "This is the time of the winds," Benigno explained as a gust shook the car. "Good for the harvest."

Yauri commands the crest of a mound in a sea of rolling hills, a town typically altiplano — the church, as in a Rivera mural, towering over the squat mud houses and neon-lit concrete plaza. A few llamas clacked along the cobbled streets, pigs encrusted themselves in the open sewers, and shawled, straw-hatted women shepherded their husbands home from the bars, swaying instinctively to the huynos shrieking from every radio.

At the police station a sergeant assured us that the road ahead was good, that we would reach Cailloma by dark. But by dark Benigno's punished sedan had carried us only seven miles. We unloaded our gear on the spiny grass beside the river, and Benigno, promising to return the following morning, headed back to town to hire a truck with enough road clearance to take us the remaining 65 miles.

Our first camp on the Apurímac. In our excitement we could ignore the frozen ground, too hard for pegs, and the drilling wind tugging at the seams of the floor where we had piled our gear to keep the tent from blowing away. Our alcohol stove soon warmed the interior, our sleeping bags were soft beneath us, and we savored the aroma of dehydrated chicken tetrazzini mixed with Apurímac water bubbling on the fire.

We awakened next morning to a world white with frost. Chipping through the ice on the Apurímac's edge I filled a pan with water; it was crusted before I reached the tent only 30 yards away. Even Balty with his thick fur coat trembled in the biting wind. And we were only at 13,000 feet. Suddenly the thought of camping at the Apurímac's 17,000-foot source lost much of its allure.

Benigno returned about nine, his round face long with gloom. He could find no one to take us to Cailloma. Perhaps, he suggested, if Helen and I went back to Yauri we could persuade someone. Returning to Yauri, I left Helen and Balty thawing in the pale sun by the market while I traced the owners of seven trucks then in town. I had no more success than Benigno: "The road is very bad," I was told, or "My battery is dead," or "It is a holiday." By the time I had talked to them all it was midafternoon, and I was about to give up and look for horses when a truck rolled by. The driver, a young Peruvian engineer with the road department, glanced at our letters of introduction from his government. With some hesitation, he agreed to take us.

"We'll be in Cailloma by dark," I announced triumphantly to Helen.

"Of which day?" she murmured, reminding me of a similar prediction the afternoon before.

Five bruising hours later, gray with dust and soggy with gasoline from a leaking drum in the back of the truck, we pulled into a dark and deserted Cailloma, a village too small to have an inn. Going in search of a place to stay, I found every door barred; highland people are suspicious of strangers after dark. Yet sometimes fortune smiles in the least-expected circumstances. From behind a shutter a voice advised me to find the gringo at the silver mine up

Huddled over an alcohol stove, Helen stirs a cup of coffee in the frosty Andean dawn. Ice crusted a pail of water as Frank carried it from the Apurímac River, only 30 yards away. Outside the tent, Indian guides load packhorses for the return trek through the roadless valley of the yet unnavigable tributary of the Amazon.

the valley. We had not known there was a gringo anywhere in the area, but my hopes soared at the word, a term used in Peru, not necessarily in derogation, to denote foreigners. Helen and I prevailed upon our exhausted young friend to take us to the mine.

Siegfried Stephan, the German-born engineer in charge, greeted us with all the aplomb of a man accustomed to receiving bedraggled strangers and an equally bedraggled dog in the middle of the night. When I stammered an introduction through chattering teeth, he replied in a voice as icy as his eyes:

"Now don't tell me you've come to discover the source of the Amazon too?"

"No, not to discover it," I replied. "I'm sure it's been known for years. But I would like to see it."

Mr. Stephan smiled. "Then come in and get warm, and we'll talk about it in the morning. The source of the Amazon is near, an easy climb. My foreman will take you there—just as he did Michel Perrin 15 years ago."

"Near" and "easy," we were to learn, even after a day of rest, are relative. Soon after dawn, with the pools of water from snow melted the afternoon before still crunchy with ice underfoot, I calibrated our altimeter to the mine's known elevation; at 14,800 feet, we were already higher than California's 14,495-foot Mount Whitney.

Mr. Stephan's truck carried us another 600 feet upward along a corkscrew mining trail. Then, with foreman Jorge Palomino Andia as guide and a burly Indian mine worker to help carry cameras, tripod, and lunch, we started up the brown, shale-littered valley. *Paja brava*—literally "wild, tough grass," its thin blades sharp as cactus—snatched at the tough cloth of our ski pants. As we climbed, even the hardy paja brava succumbed to the altitude, giving way to patches of mossy lichens and dime-size yellow blossoms draping the shaded side of the naked rock like brightly stippled green throw rugs. A condor wheeled overhead; a *viscacha,* like a marmot, whistled a warning to his mate and disappeared; only the wind coursing down the valley from the salt-white snow ridges to either side of us disturbed the quiet.

And so we climbed, trying to match the long strides of our escorts, and, failing this, pausing each 20 steps or so to catch our breath as the altimeter needle crept toward the 17,000-foot mark. In the shade now, we followed a valley where the sun probed only a few hours a day, a few months of the year;

Blind musician in the marketplace of Ayacucho, Peru, plucks the gut strings of his
altiplano harp, an instrument introduced by
Spanish settlers. At Sunday markets in
Chincheros (below), villagers barter handi-
crafts and the meager surplus of their fields.
Their limited cash they reserve for manufactured products, medicinal herbs—and for
coca, source of cocaine. Many Indians, like
the man at left, chew coca leaves mixed with
quicklime to dull hunger and fatigue; lime
and saliva act to release the numbing narcotic.

melted snow dripping from above made icicle-fanged caves of overhanging cliffs. Reaching the snow line, we scrambled up a ridge and across to the sunlit side of the twin-peaked mass called Mount Huagra—meaning "horns" in Quechua. From it issues the spring that seven name-changes and some 4,000 miles later enters the Atlantic Ocean as the Amazon.

Someday perhaps, as with the Nile, a monument will mark the source of the Amazon, and a road will lead to it. But today the world's mightiest river spawns its first drops amid silent, solitary splendor. Helen and I bent over the five-inch-wide spring seeping through the spongy, tundralike sod. We parted the green threads of moss that filtered its flow, and a small pool formed—clear and glistening in the sun. Above us the horns of Mount Huagra seemed close enough to touch. I checked the altimeter; the needle hung a line's width below 17,000 feet. We drank from the source and joked about lowering the water level of the Amazon. Helen and I had shared many adventures spanning more than half a hundred countries, and we would share many more before we reached the Atlantic. But this was the highest we had ever been outside an airplane, literally the high point of our careers. While the faces of our two companions cracked wide with grins, I bussed my wife firmly on the lips.

The Indians call this first trickle of the Amazon the Huaraco. Tracing its tumbling course down a broad valley, we watched the tiny brook grow with melting snow, turn murky yellow with mine tailings, and join a stream called the Toro to become the Santiago, which in turn becomes the Apurímac.

Before the week was out we would follow the Apurímac by horse and truck back to Yauri, and hence to Cuzco. But that day, after walking 19 miles, we could think only of being warm again. We arrived back at Mr. Stephan's home well after dark, chilled, exhausted, exhilarated. He had held dinner for us— fresh trout from his own pool—and we ate ravenously.

After a week above 14,000 feet we found the air of Cuzco positively rich with oxygen. We breathed deeply, reveling in newfound strength as we prepared for phase two of our Amazon adventure. Then with Benigno again at the wheel, we headed for the city of Ayacucho. From there a fair-weather trail led down into the jungle to San Francisco, the first town from which the Apurímac can be navigated downstream in any kind of craft. All during the two-day drive to Ayacucho, Benigno worried whether his sedan would survive the rigors of the trail trip that still lay ahead. He was much relieved when Tony Stapleton, a young British agronomist on a study tour, invited us to accompany him from Ayacucho to San Francisco in his Land-Rover.

At the pass through the last range of mountains separating us from the jungle, we looked back at the brown hills rolling westward toward the Pacific. The breeze blew fresh on our faces. We savored it, the last cool breath we would take for seven months. Then, as though offering us a parting gift, a shepherd hidden somewhere in the rocks above took up his flute. Carrying its plaintive echo of the altiplano with us, we plunged into a sea of cloud puffs floating up from the valley of the Apurímac, 8,000 feet and 30 twisting miles below.

Twisting down mist-veiled valleys between mountains cloaked in jungle, the Piene River races toward the Apurímac. Leaving the cold, arid altiplano, the Schreiders descended into the lush, humid cloud forest that flanks the Andes' eastern slopes.

Through Perilous Rapids and Whirlpools:

CHAPTER THREE

AN FRANCISCO squats on a curve of the Apurímac, 350 cascade-filled miles below its source and some 15,000 feet lower in elevation. The cleansing current rushes by the opposite bank, leaving the village's gently sloping, sandy shore littered with the dregs of nature and the debris of humanity. Pigs root in piles of garbage, and lazily circling buzzards flutter down for a morsel. Naked children skip among driftwood while short-statured Indians, some wearing tribal face stripes of red dye, transfer from canoes to trucks their crops of coca leaves, bananas, or *barbasco,* a root which yields a fish poison and an insecticide.

We were still in the Andean foothills, the so-called "high jungle," and the air was balmy. However, Helen and I, fresh from the cold altiplano, perspired freely as we strolled among the dugout canoes, balsa-wood rafts, and skiffs powered by outboard motors drawn up on the beach. In some such craft we planned to run the Apurímac. But which kind?

We needed expert advice, but we could find no one in San Francisco who knew the river farther than a few days' travel downstream. The name of one man, however, popped up over and over in our discussions with the townspeople. We headed for Hacienda Luisiana, home of Señor José Parodi O. Vargas—known to almost everyone along the Apurímac as "Pepe" Parodi.

Hacienda Luisiana lies at the end of a dirt track some eight miles upriver from San Francisco. We found Señor Parodi directing his workmen at a sugarcane press near a group of neat and substantial farm buildings.

"Señor Parodi..." I began.

"Do not call me Señor. I am Pepe." With an informality rare in Latin American gentlemen—and Pepe is every inch a gentleman—it was Pepe, Helena, and Francisco from then on.

I told Pepe where we had come from, that we wanted to travel all the way to the Atlantic using the transportation the people used, that we knew next to nothing about navigating a river like the Amazon.

Pepe pushed his hat back on his head, exposing a thatch of unruly black hair. Straight white teeth flashed in his tan, angular face. "I will speak to you frankly. You ask my advice. But if I give it, will you take it?

"I will tell you why I ask that question. You have heard of Michel Perrin? He

Awash in the Apurímac, the Schreiders' raft Mamuri *departs San Francisco for Atalaya, 250 miles downstream. During the nine-day journey, boatmen Poli (standing) and "Compadre" manned their paddles through rapids, winds, and whirlpools.*

A Message from the 'Great Speaker'

With a chonta-palm spike and a rock for a hammer, Frank christens the 7-by-20-foot balsa-wood raft, naming it after a swift Amazonian fish. "Pepe" Parodi, who warned the Schreiders of difficulties ahead, checks on conditions downriver by radio (below left). Logs stripped of their bark (below right), and then dried, formed the craft.

was advised against running the upper Apurímac. When his boat capsized in the rapids just about here, I was in the party that searched for his companion's body. I do not want to have to search for yours."

With the forceful gentleness so characteristic of him, Pepe had made his point. Subdued, we listened quietly as he outlined the problems of navigating the Apurímac. "The river is low now," he explained. "There are rapids and whirlpools, hidden rocks, submerged logs that could wreck a motorboat. A canoe is too small. Turns over too easily. You could make it on a raft—but only with an experienced riverman. I know only one man who could take you, a Campa Indian friend of mine called Policarpo. I'll send for him. But I don't know if he will agree to go."

During the two days that we waited for Poli, we began to see the high jungle as Pepe and his diminutive, energetic wife Goya saw it—a lush, almost mosquito-free garden where everything grows in profusion. With justifiable pride Pepe led us through his neat groves of coffee and cacao trees, his rows of pineapples, bananas, citrus, and *cocona,* a fruit that looks like persimmon with juice like sweet lemon and meat like an apricot. Except for wheat and potatoes brought down from the highlands, everything in the simple meals we shared with Pepe and Goya came from their 400-acre jungle farm.

Poli's first reaction to rafting down the Apurímac was negative. He had

made the trip four times as far as Atalaya, the first town from which we could continue by motorboat. It would take at least eight days to get there and a month or more to return on foot and by canoe. He did not wish to be away from his family that long.

"But you do not have to return the long way," Pepe urged. "A small plane flies to Atalaya each week. You could be back here in 12 days. Francisco will buy you a new shirt and trousers, pay all your expenses and a good salary. Poli, there is no one else I can trust to take them."

Poli's deep-set black eyes raked across my face, questioning. "I promise all that Pepe says," I told him in Spanish. What a bizarre bargain, I thought: The unlettered Campa would guide the gringos through the rapids on an Indian raft; the gringos would guarantee the Indian's return home on an airplane. For each of us the agreement represented a journey into the unknown. To Poli's unsophisticated spirit the plane trip must have seemed as much a hazard as the raft trip did to us.

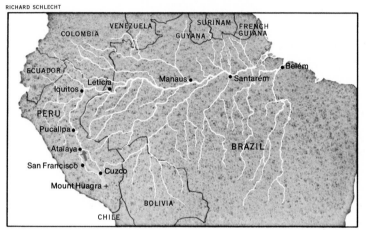

Authors Helen and Frank Schreider raft their way down the wild Apurímac, winding between walls of dense jungle.

He took my out-thrust hand, brushing my fingers gently, more a gesture than a clasp, a gesture that bound us together in solemn trust.

The bargain sealed, Pepe took a stick and scratched a rectangular outline on the ground about 20 feet long and 7 feet wide.

"The raft must be big enough to move around on but not too big to maneuver quickly," he said. He scratched a series of parallel lines running lengthwise about 7 inches apart, the average diameter of the lightweight balsa logs we would use. "Twelve logs should do it. Each will carry about 50 kilograms [110 pounds]—600 kilograms total, more than double our load." I noticed Pepe used the words "our load" and grinned to myself. We were growing very fond of this big, enthusiastic Peruvian who was making a personal project of the Schreiders' trip down the Apurímac.

Next morning Poli took us across the river in his dugout canoe to look for balsa logs. He paddled Amazon-fashion from the bow, using the swift current to help us to the other side. Carved from a single hardwood log, 12 feet long and 1½ feet wide, the canoe looked like a hollow cigar. With barely two inches of freeboard, it seemed about to capsize with every stroke of the paddle. Even Balty sensed our precarious balance; he crouched as still as a library lion in the bottom of the craft.

Though the morning breeze was still fresh on the river, the sweat rose in my pores as the jungle enveloped us. And not just from the heat. I had read too many lurid accounts of the bushmaster, fer-de-lance, and giant anaconda.

Poli led us along a path barely wide enough for a child, the vegetation on either side a Rousseau painting of ropelike vines, thorny bushes, and great gray tree trunks thrusting upward to disappear in a mass of huge, feathery ferns speckled with dancing drops of sunlight. Well ahead of us, Poli glided through the jungle like a wraith, pausing here and there to eye a balsa tree for size, moving so silently that the symphonic trill of unseen birds and insects hardly changed its pitch. As we clumped after him, twigs crackling beneath our boots, feet squishing in the damp sponge of rotting vegetation, it seemed as though the conductor had dropped his baton.

"Aren't you afraid of snakes?" Helen asked when we caught up with Poli.

His dark face brightened in a lopsided grin. "No worry," he said in his broken Spanish, "when gringo walk in jungle, snakes run away fast."

Poli quickly located 12 trees the right size, and our jungle string section gave way to a somber timpani as his machete thudded into the soft, porous balsa wood. Even after being severed from their roots, the trees remained upright, supported by nets of vines until cut free. Poli trimmed each log, stripping its thick bark in long shiny ribbons, leaving the trunk like a bolt of slick yellow satin, and we dragged them to the riverbank. Still heavy with sap, they would have to dry several days before they would float well.

With a kind of atavistic fascination, we watched the raft take form—a form as old as man's desire for transportation, older than the wheel, the sled, older even than the domestication of pack animals. The first man may have crossed his first river on a single log. From that it became a simple step to fasten two or more logs together—just as Poli was doing.

With improved tools—a steel adz instead of a flint scraper, a machete instead of a stone ax—Poli fashioned his spikes, sharpening two-foot-long spears of chonta palm, a grainy, extremely hard wood, and binding their top ends with bark so they wouldn't split. His experienced eye slanted along each log, selecting it for its curve so that the bow would turn up, and for its taper so that the raft would be narrower in front. He mated the irregularities of each log to minimize the gaps between.

Using a stone from the riverbank as a two-handed hammer, he spiked the logs together and braced them with crosspieces. With strips of soft, water-soaked bark he laced 10-foot lengths of cane to the crosspieces to make a raised floor. He arced saplings to frame a quonset-shaped roof thatched with palm fronds. He carved paddles and, at our request, mounted a pole for our National Geographic flag and added pegs on which to hang our binoculars and cameras. At the end of seven days all our craft lacked was a name.

"Why not call it *Mamuri?*" Pepe suggested with a touch of optimistic irony. "The mamuri is the fastest fish in the river."

The day of our departure dawned gray and drizzly. At the last minute Poli had decided that the raft was too big for him to handle alone, and Pepe had found another Indian to help him. He had no experience in river travel, but he assured us he could follow Poli's instructions. His Spanish name, Eulogio, tangled my tongue, so I dubbed him "Compadre"—Companion—which seemed to please him.

Or perhaps it was just the sight of our ship's larder that brought the smile to Compadre's face as we loaded the raft. On Pepe's advice we had stocked *Mamuri* with all the luxuries that Indians relish but seldom sample: cocoa, coffee, rice, noodles, sugar, oatmeal, canned milk, canned fish. If a well-fed crew made for a happy ship, *Mamuri* was off to a good start.

Society flag streaming, Mamuri *hurtles past a rock-strewn bank; Balty and Helen sit forward as Poli*

and Compadre paddle. Pepe rode through the first rapids while Frank photographed from shore.

Delayed by the rain, we did not leave until almost noon. Pepe, ever concerned for our safety, decided to check the raft through the six sets of rapids between Luisiana and San Francisco. I went ahead with Goya in the truck to photograph *Mamuri* in action from the high bluffs along the river. Helen, who remained with the raft, and I kept in touch via the tiny walkie-talkies we always carry on assignment.

The messages were disconcerting. The trail neared the river at only one set of rapids, but the sounds from the others proved graphic enough, the Apurímac talking, water boiling over rocks, a whimper from Balty as Helen grabbed him, her voice strident in spite of her efforts to remain calm: "We're entering the rapids now. *Mamuri* is tilting . . . a sunken log . . . we're going to hit it. Pepe is holding us off with a pole. Compadre is terrified . . . paddle, Compadre — paddle faster!"

Goya and I arrived in San Francisco a few minutes ahead of *Mamuri*. She rounded the bend, flag flying, victor in her first contest with the river. Helen looked pale beneath her tan, but she managed a reassuring smile. Pepe leaped ashore. Wordlessly, we shared a strong parting *abrazo* — the Latin American embrace — and I boarded *Mamuri* for the first time.

Shoving off, we soon picked up speed as Poli and Compadre steered us into the fast current in the middle of the river. Pepe and Goya escorted us the first few hundred yards in a borrowed motorboat, their *buen viaje* — good journey — ringing out over the mutter of the Apurímac.

We made camp early that day. The raft had proved harder to maneuver than we had anticipated, and Compadre was too drained by his first taste of rapids to be of much help to Poli in steering *Mamuri* through the swift current at the bends in the river. We pulled up on a driftwood-littered gravel bar, our orange tent a welcome splash of color against the gray stones set in the jungled cleft of the Apurímac Valley.

Once they had eaten, Poli and Compadre curled up around their cooking fire. With plastic sheets to keep off the night-time dew and insects, they were asleep before dusk erased the mauve dust left by the sun on the mountains soaring to each side of us. However, Helen and I were still too tense for sleep. Protected from the voracious sand flies, we lay on our cots in the insect-proof tent and listened to the piercing shrill of cicadas, unwavering except when broken by the hoarse static of a parrot's screech or the wail of a howler monkey.

The morning brought far different sounds. The gentle murmur of the river changed to an angry grumble, then a dull roar as the Apurímac narrowed and roiled between high banks. Hardly 10 minutes passed between rapids. *Mamuri* plunged through the frothing water, burying her bow, then leaping up as though to shake free from the clutching river that surged between her logs and swirled around her plastic-wrapped cargo lashed amidships.

Waves dashed over the raft, drenching us with spray and forcing us to grab the rope lifelines. We rushed along, tilting, swinging to one side, then the other as Poli and Compadre paddled frantically to keep us parallel with the swift current. Helen crouched low on the deck, gripping Balty tightly between her knees while I clutched the sun canopy with one hand and tried to grab quick pictures with the other.

But sometimes the rapids were wider. The rocky banks sloped gently away

Silent and enigmatic, Campa Indians stand before huts thatched with the leaves of caña brava, *a cane that grows along the Apurímac. Such huts—called* savoropancos *—provide temporary shelter for fishing parties who come from neighboring villages.*

from the water to where the jungle began its irregular climb toward the misty mountains that enclosed us. Occasionally the red splash of a flame tree burst through the mass of green, and here and there the spidery white skeleton of a tree trunk poked starkly from the tangle of vines that had strangled it.

At these wider places the river often split into three or four channels. Poli would stand spread-legged on the raft, trying to decide which channel to take, his hand shielding his eyes from the sun lances that ricocheted from the murky yellow water. To us, one log-choked channel looked as bad as another, and we never learned how he made his choice. When we asked him he just shrugged, "I don't know how I know. I just know."

He was wrong only once, and perhaps that was because there was so little time. Sensing the cool wind that always preceded a new series of rapids, Poli grunted orders to Compadre. They dug furiously at the water trying to swing the raft toward the outside curve, the deeper side of the river, but the current was too swift. The river split into three channels and we were swept into the middle one. We grated over a rock, scraped across a submerged log. Beneath us rumbled a low growl as the frenzied current tumbled rocks along the river bottom. *Mamuri* lurched as she struck a boulder, solidly this time, creaking with the stress. When we pulled the raft ashore to make camp that night, we found that two of the hard chonta-palm spikes had snapped off.

Next day the intervals between the rapids grew longer. *Mamuri* moved more leisurely, and the sultry air of the jungle replaced the cooling breeze of the rapids. But the Apurímac would not let us rest. A series of whirlpools snatched at the raft—great driftwood-cluttered swirls of glinting water that drew us toward the vortex and then flung us back to the periphery, only to suck us toward the center again.

Each time Poli and Compadre struggled to paddle us back into the main current. Once I tried to help, using a bamboo pole as a paddle, but lost it in the hungry water. With a frantic effort Poli urged *Mamuri* out of the whirlpool, leaving the driftwood to spin about until it became too water-soaked to float and was sucked to the bottom. I wondered how long before *Mamuri* would have followed had our companions lost their paddles as I did the pole, and we had been trapped in that swirling liquid web. I had heard that another raft and its crew had been caught in a similar whirlpool for days before escaping.

The disturbing thought lingered as we drifted downstream. Fairly strong swimmers, we might conceivably make it to shore should the raft capsize in the rapids, or should we have to abandon it in a whirlpool. But could we survive the other dangers that lurked in the water? The stingrays that can incapacitate a man for days; the electric eels that can knock him senseless; the alligatorlike caiman; the miniscule spiny *carnero* that can enter a human's smallest orifices and must be cut out; or piranhas, those dread little butcher fish that have become almost synonymous with the Amazon.

Pepe had told us that the Apurímac near Luisiana was too swift for sting-rays, eels, or piranhas. Each night when we camped, we had bathed confidently in the river and thrown sticks for Balty to retrieve.

But now the current was perceptibly slower. As we made camp that afternoon, I asked Poli if it was still safe to bathe. He assured Helen and me that we would find no eels or stingrays until well below Atalaya, that trousers were the

Versatile Poli dispatches a skewered fish with a spine-snapping crunch. He wears the rust-colored, sacklike cushma of the Campa—the tribe of his birth. At lower left, he sounds a conch shell to signal his fellow tribesmen that strangers approach. Ashore, a Campa woman brews masato, a mild intoxicant made by boiling and chewing cassava root, spitting soggy cuds into a pot, and letting the mash ferment.

best protection against carnero, that piranhas were a danger only in the more sluggish backwaters, and then only if attracted by blood.

"And caimans?" I asked, remembering the three small ones, four to six feet long, we had seen sunning themselves on a sand bar that day, looking like so many logs until they flicked into the water at our approach.

"Caimans afraid of people," Poli replied. "But no let Balty swim. Caimans like dogs to eat."

From then on we watched Balty carefully whenever he approached the water. On a black moonless night a few camps later, I heard a splash. When I played my flashlight over the water, it was as though the surface had become a mirror image of a starry sky as seen through a red filter. Like cigarettes glowing in the dark, pairs of eyes stared unblinking at my light. I understood then why caimans and crocodiles are becoming so rare along most of the Amazon, for this is how they are hunted—a powerful light, an easy target, a quick shot. I counted 11 caimans before Balty's bark frightened them away.

The slower current and the decrease in numbers of rapids indicated that the river was descending more gradually. The Apurímac Valley grew wider now, the plateau-like regions along the banks broader and more frequent. The jungle seemed to quiver with hidden life, betraying its secret with a flurry of white as a siege of herons took wing, or a streak of rust as a wild dog fled from his drinking spot at the river's edge.

We knew we were approaching Campa Indian territory when Poli donned his *cushma,* the long, cinnamon-colored gown of his tribe. He blew his conch shell, a mournful bray that echoed across the valley. In the jungle, friends usually announce their coming; enemies do not. Poli was making sure that the Campas knew we meant no harm. Still we saw no one, though we found signs aplenty—a canoe drawn up on the bank, a scattering of palm-thatch lean-tos, a fish trap made of rows of wooden tripods anchored with stones to back up the water so that the juice of the squeezed barbasco roots placed in the stream would poison the fish before being dispersed by the current. With so much evidence of habitation, the total absence of people began to unnerve us.

"They are there," Poli insisted, pointing to a pall of smoke rising from the jungle. "They are smoking wasps from a tree. Very good roasted over a fire. But the Campas know we are here. Soon they come."

Soon they did, a group of eight on a high bank. They made no move as we drifted past, not even a response to Poli's wave. Standing shoulder to shoulder in their square-cut cushmas, they might have been a string of paper dolls.

Late in the afternoon Poli beached the raft near a group of dugouts by a path leading up the steep red bank toward a village back in the jungle. Leaving us to make camp, he climbed up the trail to explain our presence to the Campas, a people once reputed to be warlike and resolute in forbidding strangers to enter their territory.

Next morning we followed Poli into the village, a random grouping of a dozen or so cane and palm-thatch huts, pale ocher in the dawn light. Drowsy sounds of a muted chorus of low voices and creaking hammocks blended with the clucking protest of a hen fleeing a rooster, the plaintive call of doves in the forest, and the rising pitch of cicadas practicing for their evening concert.

I kept Balty close beside me. When the Campa men who came to meet us saw him, they stopped in fascinated confusion until assured by Poli that we would not harm them. With polite restraint and a trace of lingering doubt — they stayed well out of Balty's leashed range — they led us into the opensided meetinghouse. We sat on a platform of split palm wood, absorbing their stares while Poli introduced us.

Cushma-clad women glided in, some carrying babies slung in shawls fringed with slivers of bone that jittered merrily as they moved. The early morning sunlight that speared the eaves turned their painted faces into Picassoesque masks of animated red triangles and squares. Their glances were curious but not unfriendly.

HOW DIFFERENT, I thought, was our reception from that given Padre Cimini, the Franciscan priest whose party of 150 armed men had been beaten back by the Campas in 1849, several miles from where we sat. Helen's thoughts must have paralleled mine. She pointed upward with her eyes. On the rafters lay a bow and a set of bamboo-bladed arrows. Beside them was a book.

For many years few Campas — fishermen, hunters, or an occasional war party — ventured near the river. Their settlements remained isolated well back in the mountain jungles. In 1948 members of the Summer Institute of Linguistics, the academic affiliate of the U. S.-based Wycliffe Bible Translators, made contact with the tribe, learned their language, and persuaded some of the youths to go to school downriver near Pucallpa. Drawn by promises of education and medical help, the Campas began to move to the Apurímac's edge, congregating in larger villages instead of remaining in single-family groups.

So far, river and jungle have prevented civilization from encroaching too rapidly on the tribe. But it is coming. Poli was just finishing his introduction when a sturdy, broad-shouldered young Campa strode into the meetinghouse, his white shirt and trousers a dazzling incongruity among the cushma-clad Indians. In Spanish, he introduced himself as the schoolteacher.

We followed the teacher to the government-owned, one-room thatch schoolhouse on the edge of the village. The students, ranging from children of five or six to youths in their late teens, joined in an uncertain rendition of the Peruvian national anthem, then settled down at the hand-hewn bench-desks for their lessons. Except for the one or two who might be selected for the Linguistics school near Pucallpa, few if any could hope for more education than the three years they received here.

Though the teacher was an "Evangélico," a Protestant convert, he hedged when we asked him his tribal name: The evil spirits that animistic Campas believe in might be listening. He dodged my questions about Campa customs except when I asked about dances.

"We do not dance any more," he said firmly. "We are Evangélicos here. We do not drink. You have to be drunk to dance well."

While Poli strengthened the raft, replacing the broken chonta-palm pegs and adding logs, we wandered freely through the village. Except for the teacher, no one spoke Spanish, and we communicated by gesture as we traded a knife for a bow and a set of arrows — a pronged arrow for frogs, barbed for fish, blunt for birds, sharp-bladed bamboo for larger game.

The day of our visit the women seemed to be engaged mainly in making *masato,* a masticated and fermented beverage the color of pale borscht, but with a somewhat less appealing flavor. Sitting by cooking fires under the overhanging eaves of their huts, they stirred blackened pots of boiling cassava root. The steam made their red makeup run like blood down their faces. While the pots cooled they brought water in gourds from the river, then washed and redid their faces, transferring geometric designs incised on a small wooden cylinder by spreading it with the oily red paste of ground *achiote* seed and rolling it across cheeks, chin, and forehead.

Once the cassava cooled, children joined their mothers around the pots. Gnawing off chunks of the starchy root, they all began to chew, spitting soggy cuds into the pots, stirring the saliva-saturated, magenta mass to the consistency of mashed potatoes. Squeezed through a basket sieve and activated by enzymes in the saliva, the masato would ferment in two or three days to a beverage with an alcoholic content equal to that of strong beer. Gourdful after gourdful was set aside to brew — a substantial quantity, I thought, for a people who did not drink. As we headed back to the raft, Helen commented, "I wonder when the dancing will begin."

A short distance below the village, the Amazon changed its name for the fourth time since its birth on Mount Huagra. Scores of smaller, rain-swollen streams had added their flow and color to the river, now glinting a silvery brown in the sun. Though the Apurímac became the Ene, it remained the Great Speaker in spirit.

It soon added wind to its vocabulary, surging gusts that moaned up the valley each afternoon, puffing out our sun canopy like a sail until *Mamuri* seemed to stop in the water. We joked about being taken back to Luisiana, but Poli just grunted, his eyes scanning the river ahead, his muscles taut and knobby as he dug his paddle deep into the current and swung us toward shore. Overwhelmed by the wind, we made an early camp on a rock-studded island.

That afternoon, with the valley bathed in a flaming sunset, Poli borrowed our bow and fishing arrows. I followed at a distance as he stalked the still pools between the rocks, his cushma glowing a vivid coral, his eyes somehow divining the mottled water. He drew the bow, aiming a bamboo-barbed arrow at a pool some 30 feet away. I could see nothing, not even a shadow among the boulders, but Poli could. With an instinct as precise as an artillery computer, he gauged trajectory, water refraction, and angle of entry. The bowstring flicked, the arrow skimmed low across the water, so low I thought it would skip from the surface like the flat stones I used to throw as a boy. A flash of silver stirred the amber pool, and Poli dashed forward to grab a foot-long fish spitted on the arrow. Raising the fish to his mouth he crushed its backbone with his teeth, and the thrashing creature became still.

Here, I thought, stood basic man, superbly adapted to his environment. I wondered how long Helen and I — or even Balty, city-bred as he was — would survive were we forced to fend for ourselves in this forest where only the practiced eye can even see a fish, where only the initiated can distinguish the edible plants from the poisonous ones, where the jungle tolerates man but provides comparatively little from its own larder to sustain him.

The stretch known as the Ene marks the final *(Continued on page 77)*

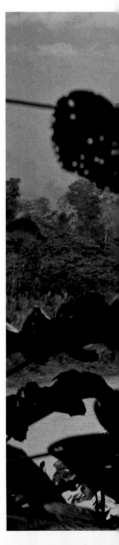

Gathering waters feed a growing river. Some 1,100 major tributaries and countless trickles, like "Linguistic Waterfall" and the Shinipo (above), help to swell the Amazon. Below, Mamuri drifts on the Apurímac below forests of the Vilcabamba range.

Ready for class, Machiguenga Indian children form ranks in their jungle-rimmed schoolyard at Monte Carmelo, a village on the Urubamba River. The Summer Institute of Linguistics—an affiliate of the U.S.-based Wycliffe Bible Translators—trains teachers and assists in operating schools in isolated areas of the Amazon.

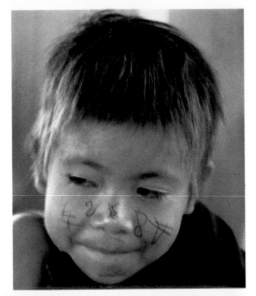

Young Campa girls—dressed in the traditional cushma—practice their letters in a school at Quimpiri. Another (at top) wears facial decorations playfully applied by classmates. Indians of the Amazon Basin have undergone varying degrees of acculturation: These Campas lived in widely scattered huts and had practically no village life until missionaries established the school. About 75 families have now settled nearby.

Under a low-hanging morning mist, Helen splashes her face with cool water. The Schreiders found such quiet coves a welcome respite after long days of battling white water and whirlpools. Between its source and Atalaya, the river drops 16,000 feet.

HELEN AND FRANK SCHREIDER

stage in the Amazon's precipitous descent. The confining mountains, which had seen the first drop seeping from Mount Huagra grow to a river almost as long and as wide as the Rhine, seemed to lean toward each other in one last attempt to pinch off the flow, to prevent it from spilling out onto the vast flatland of jungle and swamp that is the Amazon Basin.

Boiling through gray canyons of stone, around house-size boulders, past banks so steep the tree roots clung like spiders to the red earth, the Ene swept us through the rapids of Paquipachango and Utica, the last barriers to small-boat navigation up the Amazon. The mountains retreated, the Ene broadened, and the Amazon changed its name for the fifth time to become the Tambo.

Just before the entrance to the Tambo, the Great Speaker delivered his parting remarks. All morning we had raced along on a current varying between an estimated 5 and 12 miles per hour. We were sure we would get through the stone canyon that rose wall-like to either side of us before the afternoon wind came up, but the first gust caught us well inside. Blast after blast snatched at our sun canopy, splintering the frame and crackling the palm-frond thatch, reeling us back against the current.

Poli and Compadre urged us along with the paddles, searching vainly for a break in the steep banks to beach the raft. By the time the Perené merged with the Ene to form the Tambo, our friends had become too sapped to avoid the brown maelstrom at the junction. Robbed of energy and will by three hours of battling the wind, they sat wilted on the stern as the *Mamuri* spun sickeningly toward the vortex of a block-wide whirlpool.

Grabbing a paddle, I scrabbled ineffectually at the water, working to slow our dizzy spinning, hoping that Helen could coax Poli or Compadre to try again. Time after time I fought toward the edge of the swirl only to be driven back by the wind. Blinded by sweat, the strength ebbing from my arms, I felt the raft lurch toward the vortex, then straighten as Poli added his force to mine, paddling hunched beside me while Helen called the strokes like a coxswain. We concentrated on savage digs at the water, lunging forward between gusts and holding our own when the wind blew. Slowly, so slowly, we moved across the ring of foam at the edge of the whirlpool and into the current again.

"Today very bad," Poli said as we tried to catch our breath. "But soon no more rapids, no more whirlpools. Soon we reach Atalaya."

I hoped he was right. The six days since we had left Luisiana had begun to weigh heavily on us. Like tattered, battered *Mamuri,* we did not sail jauntily along any more, nor bounce back from the daily round of rapids and whirlpools. The constant wind aggravated a gnawing tension, and the nightly rain drummed through our sleep. Despite repellent, the insects had been feasting for the last two days; we were covered with welts from sand flies and mosquitoes and black flies that bit through our clothes and left signatures in droplets of blood.

In the increasingly humid heat we felt capable of doing little more than ticking off the miles on the map as we floated downstream. I began to think of Atalaya as something that lay at the end of a rainbow. And so it seemed on the ninth day when Poli blew his conch shell for the last time, and we sighted a cluster of rusty metal roofs, bright as Campa cushmas drying in the sun. The river, now called the Ucayali, flowed off into the haze beyond—broad, brown, shiny, and, best of all, silent.

A Conflict of Divergent Cultures: Indian

DURING THE LONG DAYS of fighting rapids and whirlpools, we had imagined Atalaya—a village of 1,000 inhabitants—as a busy river port aswarm with painted Indians dickering with traders up from Pucallpa. In momentary flights of fancy we visualized ourselves cruising down the Ucayali sprawled on a bundle of jaguar skins, with the odors of sarsaparilla and barbasco roots, half-cured caiman and boar hides, and pungent black balls of smoked wild rubber all blending into a heady jungle aroma. Instead, the only painted face we found was one of a Chinese movie star on a barroom calendar and the lone forest product a stack of wild pigskins in the general store. When we finally located an outboard-powered dugout canoe for the four-day trip to Pucallpa, we sat on our bedrolls, squeezed between a drum of gasoline and a case of beer.

What our transport lacked in romantic cargo, it more than made up for in peace of mind. After the varying voice of the Apurímac, the steady hum of the motor was a song of reassurance, and our boatman Raúl swung us swiftly along the invisible channel with the skill of a man born to the river. We settled back to enjoy the fleeting palette of matted jungle and blue skies, *café au lait* water, and cotton-white clouds.

Soaring mist-gray mountains had given way to a flat jungle blanket that stretched as far as we could see. The silver gleam of the Apurímac rapids had smoothed to a sepia mirror, and somber-hued sand bars had replaced the rocks and gravel banks that had glared so blindingly in the sun. Bled of energy by its final dash for freedom from its prison of mountains, the river flowed placidly off before us. In the 600 miles from its source the stream had dropped 16,000 feet. From here to the Atlantic, a distance of 3,600 miles, it would fall only another 700 feet. Ahead of us stretched the 2.3-million-square-mile green world of the Amazon Basin—a largely unexplored, undeveloped, and virtually uninhabited jungle.

For reasons that we discovered painfully the first night we camped, this part of the Ucayali is known as the "mosquito river." More populated than the Apurímac, it flows between steep red banks spotted with cane-and-thatch settlements and an occasional miniature of Atalaya. Where hardwood trees have been timbered out along the river's edge, the jungle is lower—a dark, riotous growth

Shimmering beneath a papaya-shrouded sun, the Ucayali River flows into an immense jungle realm 2/3 the size of the 50 United States. By missionary count, 212 Indian tribes live in the thinly populated Amazon Basin—many in virtually inaccessible areas.

Tribes in a Modern World

Fresh from a cooling river bath, a Shipibo woman wraps herself in a hand-loomed skirt appliquéd with intricate rectilinear designs; below, she nestles her young daughter. The artistic Shipibos live in villages and family settlements along the Ucayali.

Fondness for geometric motifs carries over into Shipibo pottery (below). Among the villagers, the authors found graphic evidence of the impact of education—some potters now embellish their wares with numbers and letters of the alphabet.

HELEN AND FRANK SCHREIDER

patched by the shimmering emerald of wild-banana groves and the green velvet of mineral-poor natural pastures that barely support the corduroy-ribbed cattle grazing there. Raúl told us that a few Peruvians are moving in to raise rice, beans, peanuts, or watermelons on sand bars exposed at extreme low water. Some also grow cotton, corn, and oranges on the higher ground back from the river. But we saw no sign of activity on the drab farms along the way. Life on the Ucayali seemed gripped by a heat-induced coma.

Often, when Raúl pulled ashore to transfer gasoline from the drum to the motor's smaller tank, we wandered back to Shipibo Indian villages hidden in glens of banana, cassava, mango, and papaya. Like bright birds, the women retreated laughingly before us, their ruffled blouses and appliquéd skirts splashing primary colors on the green canvas of the forest.

Sometimes, if we arrived in the morning when it was cooler, we found the women weaving cloth on the raised, split-palm platforms of open-sided thatch huts. Others made pottery, using the most ancient technique known, smoothing spiraled ropes of clay to the desired shape. Ornamented with intricate geometric designs of colors extracted from barks, roots, and earth, kilned in pits of glowing charcoal, the forms ranged from fine, thin-walled masato bowls to huge potbellied urns with faces, ears, and hands, used for storing grain.

At first glance from the river, Pucallpa takes on the appearance of a heap of scrap metal piled on a flow of glowing lava with an army of monstrous water beetles scurrying at its edge. As we drew nearer, the scrap metal resolved into ranks of oddly angled corrugated roofs in various stages of oxidation. The red streaks on the high banks that had looked like lava became the detritus of the dozen or so lumber mills that dump their sawdust into the river. And the water beetles turned into an incredible assemblage of small powerboats, rafts, and canoes, none of which presented much hope of habitability for the next phase of our journey down the Amazon to Iquitos.

Raúl maneuvered the canoe into a backwater scummed with crude oil and sewage and tied up between a barge loaded with panting cattle and a house-raft of Shipibo women. Reluctant to unload our gear on the refuse-slippery shore, I wandered off through a mud-flat maze of shacks and bars looking for a conveyance to take us to a hotel. I hoped there was more to Pucallpa than the portal I was seeing.

Happily there was. From a town of 5,000 in 1940, Pucallpa has exploded to a thriving city of 60,000 people. "A war baby," one old-timer explained. Nudged by the need for natural rubber during World War II, vitalized by the Trans-Andean Highway pushed through from Lima, stimulated by a small oil strike nearby and construction of a refinery that provides the cheapest fuel on the river, Pucallpa has become the boomtown of the Peruvian Amazon.

A plywood and a paper mill exploit the abundant resources of the forest. An outboard-motor assembly plant and an aluminum-speedboat works satisfy much of the local demand for rapid river transportation. Up to 300 trucks a week bring everything from barbed wire to baby buggies from the Pacific Coast. With Peru's preferential tariffs for jungle regions, the pioneer British shipping line—Booth Steamship Company, Ltd.—brings canned goods from England to sell in its own supermarket at prices lower than those in Lima. There is even an ice-cream parlor serving American-style hamburgers and malts.

The net result has been both boom and burden. With no sewers, wells are contaminated. With no water-treatment plant, drinking water is carted in cans from distant wells and delivered to homes on transport ranging from bicycles to horse carts. Trucks churn the unpaved streets into a wallow of mud or a blizzard of dust, depending on the rains, and the electric power plant is about as dependable as a candle in a hurricane.

To Helen and me, Pucallpa ranks as the ugliest town of its size on the Amazon. But it is also the most colorful, with all that we had fondly imagined Atalaya would offer—warehouses stacked with jaguar and wild boar hides, macaw-bright Indians selling beads in the street, and trading boats with cargoes of monkeys, snarling ocelots, and parrots as vivid as oil slicks.

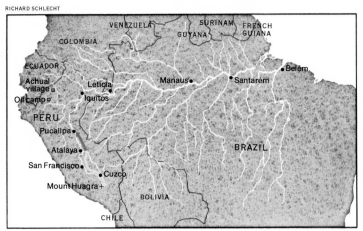

Frank flies northwest from Pucallpa to an oil-drilling site, then visits an Achual village at the edge of the modern world.

In hope of arranging a visit with one of the more remote Indian tribes of the Peruvian Amazon before setting off downriver again, Helen and I approached the Summer Institute of Linguistics, whose effect among the Campas we already had seen along the Apurímac.

The institute's base at Yarinacocha, 10 miles out of town, seemed an island of serenity in contrast to the hurly-burly of Pucallpa. Located on a lovely black-water lake, one of hundreds continually forming all along the Amazon when the river's changing course cuts off an oxbow bend, Yarinacocha offers a bit of Americana in the jungle.

Rambling bungalows, each designed, built, and paid for by the missionaries themselves, lie scattered in groves of trees. Schools, a hospital, cafeteria, and commissary provide for the 65 missionary families, mostly American, and the 140 Peruvian employees. The base even has its own water-treatment plant, electric and telephone systems, and complete maintenance facilities for its fleet of planes ranging from single-engine Cessnas to a Catalina amphibian of World War II vintage.

Painted in large letters on the hangar by the airstrip were the initials JAARS. We asked Jerry Elder, the institute's director of tribal affairs, what the letters stood for.

"Jungle Aviation and Radio Service," he replied. "We're a service as well as a missionary organization. In some parts of the jungle we're the only contact the people have with civilization. We fly rescue missions and bring the seriously sick to hospitals. To offset some of our expense, we carry cargo and passengers to isolated areas that lack other transportation.

"But the main duty of JAARS is to supply our linguists in the jungle. These linguists work with Indian tribes, analyzing their unwritten languages, developing basic alphabets, preparing simple reading texts, and translating other books, including the Bible, into tribal dialects. We may have as many as 25 couples, some with children, among the tribes at any one time."

"How do we pay for all this? The Peruvian Government helps by supplying some of our aviation gasoline and by financing all of the Indian teacher-training program. But most of our funds come from charitable organizations and churches throughout the world, especially the States. Each linguist must raise his own money by giving lectures during his home leave and through continued contact with donors by mail. Not even our pilots are paid."

The institute's dedicated pilots are among the finest I've ever flown with. Early one morning, while Helen reluctantly remained behind in Pucallpa to search for a boat to take us to Iquitos, I boarded the beautifully maintained, 25-year-old Catalina for a flight to an American oil-drilling site on the Santiago River, a tributary of the Marañón.

My mission was twofold: to see how air support has revolutionized the search for oil in the jungle, and to share, however briefly, the life of a linguist family among the Achual Indians, a tribe related to the famed Jivaro head-hunters, near the Peru-Ecuador frontier.

The gray overcast that had clouded my hopes for aerial photographs had broken by the time the Catalina reached its cruising altitude of 5,000 feet. From the plexiglass observation bubbles where machine gunners once stood, I studied the muddy river, a golden serpentine ribbon in the early morning light. The oxbow lakes that bordered it punctuated the landscape like dark commas, their waters cleared of silt and dyed black with decaying vegetation. Some already had been reclaimed by the jungle, each a light-green scar fringed with the brown freckles of isolated huts. As we turned away from the river, even these blemishes vanished. Only unbroken jungle lay beneath us.

"I always get a funny feeling when we leave the river," said a voice beside me. George Woodward, the Lingüístico pilot, had come back to chat. "When we're near water, chances are we could land if anything went wrong. But if we went down in that stuff, the jungle would close right over us. We'd never be found. I don't suppose anyone really knows what's down there. Nothing, probably. No villages, no people, nothing."

The five-hour flight that day was fertilizer for the tiny seed of doubt that had sprouted in my mind as Helen and I floated down the Apurímac, uncertain whether we could survive by ourselves in the forest, knowing that people unacquainted with the region have starved to death on the Amazon ever since the days of Orellana.

Was this fecund jungle unfolding beneath me really the hope of South America, the breadbasket and new frontier for the millions already straining the agricultural resources of the more developed areas of the continent? Government officials, many journalists, even some scientists maintain that it is. They point out that in all the Amazon Basin the population density averages only two persons per square mile. And, they add, most of these people are concentrated along the navigable rivers, leaving the remainder of the vast region virtually uninhabited.

All that empty land, boosters of the Amazon claim, could support the future millions of Latin Americans, a people who are increasing at the fastest rate in the world. And the soil—how fertile it must be to grow jungle so thick one must cut his way through it. The Amazon Basin, they conclude, could solve most of the food problems of the world, or at least those of Latin America.

All this and more I had heard and read many times. But if it is true, why are peasants from the altiplanos pouring into Lima slums at the rate of a thousand a week when the Peruvian Government offers them free land in the Amazon jungle, when government incentives and U. S. aid projects are doing everything possible to make this land attractive and accessible? Why is the diet of those already living along the Amazon among the poorest in the world? Why cannot these people feed even themselves in their almost empty land? Why has every effort toward large-scale food production in the Amazon Basin failed?

These questions had troubled me ever since Cuzco, where I had met the eminent tropical agriculturist, William C. Paddock, co-author of several books and papers on the subject. The immense carpet of green that stretched below me brought to mind a passage from his book, *Hungry Nations:*

"Agronomists have already demonstrated that of all the soils of the world, that of a rain forest is perhaps the poorest nutritionally. The huge trees keep alive merely from the sun, from the excessive rainfall and from their self-made compost piles of leaves, which guard the soil's attenuated supply of nutrients."

"Strip away this jungle growth," Dr. Paddock had told me, "as has so often been tried around the Equator, and without extreme cost and care a crop cannot be grown longer than a couple of years. Until research finds the way, failure is the fate of most farmers entering the jungle with today's seeds and tools."

Some more-suitable tools and seeds *are* available, but not at a cost that individuals—or even governments—can afford on a large scale. As the Catalina bucked and swerved around black thunderheads, I recalled another jolting ride I had had a few days earlier. Steve Stoltzfus, resident manager for machinery at the million-acre Tournavista Project near Pucallpa, had demonstrated a jungle-crushing monster developed by the late American philanthropist-industrialist R. G. LeTourneau. Protected by a steel cage atop the machine, we had moved through virgin jungle at four miles an hour. The crusher's giant boom toppled 150-foot-high trees; its knife-bladed rollers, 6 feet in diameter, ground smaller growth to splinters, clearing a 26-foot-wide swath.

"You see," Steve said enthusiastically, "we've solved the problem of clearing the jungle. Now we have to find something that will grow and return a profit."

Jute, pepper, cashew and Brazil nuts have been returning a sporadic profit along the Amazon for years. Better cover crops are being developed and cattle seemed to be thriving at the Tournavista Project. But this is not enough. To date no basic food crop has been found that will grow productively for long in the leached Amazon soil without prohibitively expensive fertilizing.

Before we reached the mouth of the Amazon, Helen and I were to conclude that the optimists who look to the Amazon Basin to feed the hungry millions of the future will look in vain unless a major breakthrough in tropical agriculture is realized. In none of the experimental stations that we visited along the Amazon were we given even a hint that such a breakthrough is in sight.

This is not to say that the Amazon Basin lacks potential riches. However,

Wary but curious, Mayoruna Indians of eastern Peru survey a missionary jungle camp. This initial encounter, in August 1969, climaxed six years of efforts by the Summer Institute of Linguistics to establish contact with the tribe. Palm splinters adorn upper lips of the young men; one wears a shirt, a gift from the Lingüísticos.

except for the great stands of timber, most of this wealth lies *beneath* the soil. Gold, diamonds, emeralds, coal, bauxite, iron, and manganese have been discovered. But so far only the last three have been found in deposits rich enough to be exploited on a commercial scale.

The search for oil continues. But not by machete-wielding crews like those who brought in the first strike many years ago near Pucallpa. Beneath our wings along a high bank of the Santiago River suddenly appeared the Fortaleza camp of Mobil/Union Group, Mobil Oil-operated, a consortium of American companies. The camp's aluminum, air-conditioned dormitories and warehouses rose from a clearing as smooth as a golf course.

"Not much time for golf," John Pittman, logistics superintendent, replied in answer to my comment. "We're spudding in at a new site. We've drilled three wells in this area so far. All dry. But we figure we'll bring oil out of one hole in ten. In the old days we could never move around this much. But with helicopters we can shut down our rig and be drilling again at another site miles away in 17 days. Not bad considering we have to take down, move, and set up again almost 600 tons of equipment. We'll run out to the rig after lunch."

An hour later, the sleek, bubble-nosed jet helicopter darted up like a dragonfly and clattered off toward the drill site some 20 miles away. In as many minutes we were over the area, the tall drill rig towering like some surrealistic tree in the jungle. A larger helicopter was lifting a piece of heavy equipment to ferry to the new site.

"Two tons' worth," our pilot said. "It takes 294 trips to move the whole outfit. Drilling would be impossible without these whirlybirds."

On the way back to camp, Mr. Pittman pointed out a series of clearings in the jungle, each about a hundred yards in diameter and ringed by felled trees. "Making those clearings is the first step in setting up a rig. Emergency landing pads. We have them along every flight path, three miles apart. That's about as far as we figure a man can find his way in that jungle. Except the Indians, of course. You know, we've had Jivaro types—feathers, blowguns, and all—working for us. Imagine, riding in a helicopter when they've never even seen a car."

At noon the next day Lingüístico pilot Ed Lind picked me up at Fortaleza in a single-engine Cessna floatplane. Crewcut and blond, he looked less like a missionary than a football player—a tired football player. For two days he had been flying from dawn to dusk ferrying linguists and their families back to the base at Yarinacocha, where they would spend the approaching rainy season compiling their notes and translating sections of the Bible into tribal dialects.

"I thought of being a commercial pilot once," Ed told me as the small plane cruised east, sandwiched in clear air between dark jungle below and darker cloud layers above. "But while I was in college I changed my mind. I figured this was what God wanted me to do."

God must have wanted him to keep right on doing it, judging by the landing he made on the tiny Huasaga, a tributary of the Pastaza River, in turn a tributary of the Marañón and the Amazon. Little more than a creek, the Huasaga was barely as wide as the wingspan and as twisty as a mountain road. Dropping below treetops into the narrow corridor cut by the stream, following its curves like a sports-car driver, Ed settled the Cessna on the water, pulled up to miss a floating log, settled again, and taxied toward a clearing on the bank where a

Signaling that they come in peace, Achual Indians blare through shotgun barrels as they approach a neighboring settlement. A drink of masato (below) reaffirms a friendship. Born of years of intertribal warfare, the ritual survives in an era of missionary influence; Achual attire also bespeaks cultural transition.

Pressing his lips to the throat of a woman dying of tuberculosis, an Achual brujo, *or shaman, tries to suck out a "spirit dart" she believes makes her ill. A few yards away villagers (right) gather for a Christian prayer meeting attended by missionaries Ruby and Gerhard Fast, seated at left with daughter Monica and pilot Ed Lind. "If only I did not have to leave now," Mr. Fast said as he prepared to fly back to Lingüístico headquarters near Pucallpa where he would spend the rainy season translating the Bible into Achual. "I feel some of these people are almost ready to receive the word of God."*

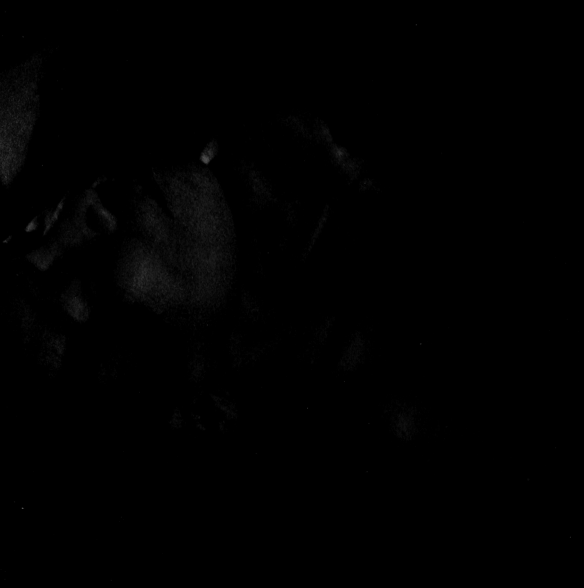

crowd of Achual Indians had gathered. A few of the men wore brilliant red
and yellow crowns of toucan feathers, some carried blowpipes or shotguns, but
most wore khaki pants and shirts; the women stood draped in shapeless shifts
of faded cotton prints. They all stared impassively as a tall, balding, ascetic-
looking man waded out to meet us.

Gerhard Fast speaks English with a slight German accent, his wife Ruby
with a Southern one. Their blond, three-year-old, elfin daughter Monica speaks
a mixture of English, Spanish, and Achual. She comes by this facility easily.
Born in Peru of an American mother and a German-Peruvian father, she has
spent most of her short life playing with Achual children in this village where
her parents have chosen, as they put it, "to spread the word of God."

Later, as we ate a simple meal of boiled cassava, fried bananas, and stewed
chicken in their palm-thatch hut, I asked the Fasts why they did not bring in
a kerosene refrigerator—or at least an oil stove to use for cooking instead of
the wood fire that glowed on the dirt floor and filled the air with smoke.

"Because we want to live as simply as possible so that our standard of living
will not be too high above that of the Indians," Gerhard replied.

"Well, why not build a more substantial house with screens to keep out the
insects? And make cots strung with rope instead of sleeping on hard split-palm
platforms. That would not be ostentatious. The materials are in the jungle. The
Indians could help, and they would learn by example how to improve their
own standard of living."

"The Indians are quite conservative," Gerhard explained. "They will not
change their way of life overnight. So we must live as they do, not set ourselves apart from them. We must gain their confidence, learn their language
and customs, teach them to read the scientific alphabet we have developed so
they can read the Bible when we translate it into their dialect. It has taken a
long time, but at last the chief is becoming interested."

I lingered behind to write my notes while the Fasts went ahead to attend a
prayer meeting. Through the cracks in the split-palm walls I watched the
Achuals throng off to the meetinghouse in the jungle several hundred yards
away. Alone in the village, I scribbled by the wavering light of a wick lamp,
shadows from my hand flitting like bats across the thatch roof.

I wrote a long time. Then, suddenly, I felt my hair bristle. When I brushed it
back with my hand, I touched feathers, and when I turned my head I almost
turned the table over in fright.

Only inches from my face stood an Achual brave in full headhunting regalia,
his red-smeared face like a mask in the lamp's feeble flame. Feather-tufted
tubes of bamboo protruded from his earlobes. A quiver of darts hung at his
waist and his eight-foot blowpipe almost touched the thatch overhead. No
shrunken heads, but the tufts of hair and feathers hanging in ropes down his
chest were ominous enough. I don't know how long he had been standing
there, fascinated by my squiggles, but somehow I had no more to write.
Together we strolled off to the prayer meeting.

I found the meetinghouse lighted by tiny oil lamps held by some of the
women, each an island of orange in the darkness. Ed Lind and the Fasts sat on
benches at one side of the thatched, open shed, the Achuals on ranks of other
benches around the edges. The women cradled suckling babes, the men their

Wrestling their dugout canoe along a slippery, moss-covered bank, Tucanoan Indians portage around Yuruparí Cachivera — Devil's Cataract — on the black-water Vaupés River in Colombia. Such rapids limit navigation on many northern headwaters. In contrast to the murky Amazon, these tributaries flow over rocky beds, remaining free of silt. But decaying vegetation discolors their waters — hence the name black-water.

LOREN McINTYRE

Finger-size characins leap as high as 4 feet as they vault Vaupés River rapids in their struggle upstream to spawn (opposite). At the peak of a run, traps made from vines and reeds may yield catches like the one at left in a few minutes.

shotguns. Resplendent in a magnificent feather headdress and brilliantly white shirt and trousers, the chief stood out from all the others. Gerhard was speaking gently in Achual, his low voice asking them, he told me later, to remember God's word while he was away. He bowed his head, the Achuals did likewise, and he prayed. He led them in a new hymn, the mumbled words of the tribesmen more a chant superimposed on a familiar melody.

"There is so much to do back at the base — my language analysis and translations," Gerhard told me later. "If only I did not have to leave now. I feel some of these people are almost ready to receive the word of God."

Perhaps some are, and with the Fast family's compassionate patience I'm sure many will one day. But in the past the greatest resistance to evangelism in the jungle has come from the *brujos,* or witch doctors, who see the missionaries' modern medicines as a threat to their livelihood. I asked Gerhard how influential they were in his village.

"Not very," he replied, "though some people still rely on them. There's one here now treating a woman who's dying of tuberculosis. We tried to help her, but she's too far gone, so she called in the brujo. Come along; you will be interested. Like most Indians in this part of the jungle, the Achuals believe that illness is caused by invisible darts shot into the body by a brujo. If another witch doctor can find that dart and suck it out, the Indian is encouraged that he will recover. Often he does."

We found the woman, emaciated from her long illness, stretched on a low platform in a hut near the river. An Achual man, in shirt and trousers, disappointingly nondescript for a witch doctor, stood over her, drawing deeply on a crudely rolled cigarette.

"A kind of green tobacco," Gerhard whispered. "Very strong."

The brujo stirred a dark liquid in a glass and tossed it down in one gulp.

"*Ayahuasca,* a hallucinatory drug. Combined with the green tobacco it produces a trancelike state."

We waited about 20 minutes for the drug to take effect, the brujo weaving and chanting over his patient the whole time, the woman lying apathetically under a dirty white cloth, little beads of sweat rolling down her cheeks, the whole scene eerily medieval in the faint glow of an oil lamp. The brujo moved closer to his patient until his lips were touching her throat. After a moment he raised his head, his eyes rolled back, his mouth opened.

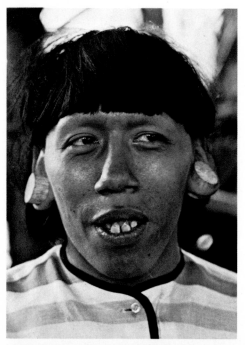

Missionary-linguist Rachel Saint fights for the lives and the souls of Auca Indians who speared her brother and four other American missionaries to death in 1956. Three years later Miss Saint made contact with the Aucas, a remote Ecuadorian tribe; she has lived and worked with them ever since. With two of her brother's killers — now converted to Christianity — beside her, Miss Saint cares for a youth stricken with polio (opposite). As she tilts the specially designed hammock downward, the patient's internal organs press against his diaphragm, forcing air from his lungs; tilting it upward helps him to inhale. The hammock hangs in the shade beneath the chapel (the oval-roofed building at right, below) of the Tiwaeno River settlement. The Auca man at left wears balsa earplugs, a tribal custom said to ensure marital fidelity.

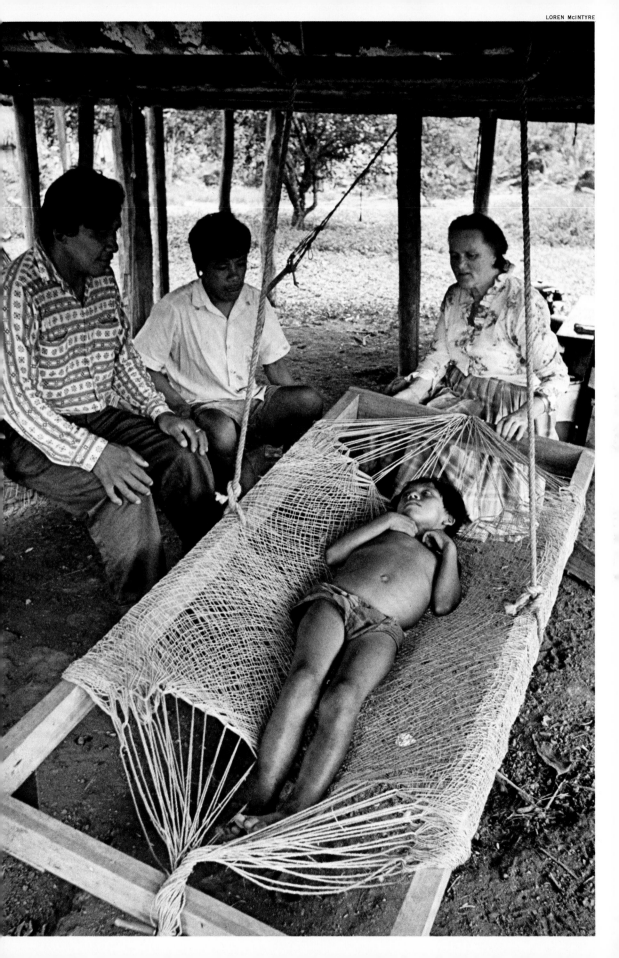

He didn't get the dart. While I watched, the brujo repeated the procedure several times, but without success. He would keep trying all night long, and possibly for three nights running. However, in this case I doubted that he would ever "succeed," for brujos are skilled natural psychologists as well as great showmen. The brujo knew the woman was dying; if he pretended to extract the imaginary dart and the woman failed to recover, his reputation would be damaged.

Back at the Fasts' hut, I asked about the jungle medicines and herbs Amazon Indians are reputed to use so effectively. I knew that pharmaceutical companies were doing extensive research on jungle remedies, that Indians had first treated malaria with quinine, used coca as a pain-killer, that modern doctors had found curare, the poison used on darts and arrows, useful in controlling spasms. Did the Achual brujos have any special medicines?

"Some, I suppose," Gerhard replied, "but they're secretive about them."

"They're not so secretive about one treatment," Ruby added. "Don't be alarmed by the sound of retching you'll hear in the morning. A gallon or so of *wayus,* a tealike stimulant, on waking makes an effective emetic. The Achuals believe that a good clearing of the stomach starts the day off right."

The retching noises did nothing to start *my* day off right. But then I hadn't slept very well anyway. I kept dreaming of that painted face over my shoulder and a fist-size head with sewn lips and eyes and long hair. It was mine. I was glad to awaken among *ex*-headhunters.

All along the Amazon, we were to learn, intertribal blood revenge and headhunting are on the wane. Once the Indian puts aside his weapons, the boat-borne itinerant trader comes. Each time he visits he takes away with him a few more of the trappings of tribal culture. For who will bother to handloom fabrics when the trader gives factory cloth in exchange for a jaguar or a caiman skin? Who will mold clay into pottery or weave baskets when aluminum pots or plastic buckets can be had for a bundle of barbasco roots or a lump of smoked wild rubber?

Worse, too many traders exploit the Indian's innate sense of honor and his inability to comprehend numbers. Persuading the Indian to take goods on credit, charging inflated prices for his baubles, and giving less than value for the jungle products in return, the trader keeps the Indian in virtual slavery trying to pay off a debt that never diminishes. So it was a hundred years ago; so it is today.

Like many journalists, anthropologists, and tourists, I had long resented the detribalization, the loss of culture and arts that has always gone hand-in-hand with missionary work, no matter how strongly the missionaries protest that such is not their intention. But on the long flight back to Pucallpa, I found that resentment softening. I could see that with more and more of the Amazon Basin opening, with mines and sawmills demanding more and more labor, the Indian must acquire at least the basic knowledge of reading and writing, adding and subtracting—knowledge that only missionary resources and patience seem capable of providing with any consistency.

With or without the missionaries, the Indian's culture appears doomed. Missionaries may be bringing on his assimilation a little more quickly, but they also are making it somewhat less painful.

*Shipibo Indians fish at dawn from a canoe on placid Lake Yarinacocha near Pucall-
pa, Peru. Each day along the Amazon brings new incursions of a 20th-century world.
In some Indian tribes, new ways meld with old; in others, the old ways wither and die.*

LOREN McINTYRE

97

Aboard Amazon Queen: Navigating an

ACK IN PUCALLPA, I joined Helen in quest of a way downriver to Iquitos. The few craft making the Pucallpa-Iquitos run travel day and night, stopping — if at all — at only a few of the villages along the way. We wanted to go at our own pace, to explore the narrow tributaries and lagoons, to learn to know the Amazon intimately.

If only we had our own boat. However, the few we found for sale looked as if they should have been scrapped, not sold — rotten-planked hulks kept afloat, seemingly, only by accumulations of greasy residue in their bilges. A new craft appeared to be out of the question. On the Amazon all boats are built to order, a process that takes months for even the simplest design. But one leaf-filled hull lying under a mango tree at the edge of town excited us every time we passed. Although it lacked cabin, decking, motor, propeller, and rudder, the most time-consuming piece of construction — the hull — had been completed except for caulking.

Made of well-seasoned *cedro,* or Spanish cedar, it looked sturdy enough to weather the ocean-size waves on the lower Amazon. Thirty feet long and seven feet at the beam, it would be big enough to live on yet small enough for us to handle by ourselves. With its shallow draft — about two feet, we guessed — we could pull up to shore wherever the swift tropical twilight found us. In a boat like this. . . . We cast the thought aside. The rainy season would be upon us before anything similar could be constructed.

"Not so," the builder, a Peruvian-Chinese, told us. "You can have this one. The man who ordered it ran out of money. I can finish the caulking, decking, and cabin in two weeks."

We could hardly believe our luck. Nor could Annelore and Heinz Maulhardt, our German hosts at the hotel. Longtime residents of the area, they warned us, "Nothing works that fast in Pucallpa. You'll be lucky to finish in twice that time."

They were right. Though the boatbuilder completed his work as promised, there was so much more to do. Perfectionists, Helen and I drew detailed plans with precise measurements. Believing in the philosophy of *mas o menos,* more or less, the carpenters squared corners by eye, and used *brazos,* the length of two outstretched arms, for large measurements, and *dedos,* the width of a finger,

Rivermen strain against the sweeps of their raft as they float a cargo of bananas down the broadening Ucayali. From Pucallpa to the sea — 3,240 miles distant — the Schreiders traveled by boat, navigating through a maze of constantly shifting channels.

Ever-Changing Waterway

for smaller ones. When windows that should have been square became trapezoids and the mechanics installed the propeller shaft 15 degrees off-center, Helen and I took up the tools ourselves. Somehow construction progressed.

"Peruano on the outside, Americano on the inside," a spectator commented as we added bunks with mattresses stuffed with kapok from the jungle, tables and benches of plywood from the local factories, screens to keep out insects, shutters to keep out rain, and a glassed-in wheelhouse to keep out waves. We put in a bucket toilet, then a shower fed from a 50-gallon oil drum pressurized with a tire pump and filled with rainwater channeled from the roof. Our navigation lamps, interior lights, and fans operated off a six-volt battery charged by an automobile generator.

For our main power I would have preferred a marine diesel, but those available were either too big or too small for our boat. Instead, we selected the engine most commonly used on this part of the Amazon, a 12-horsepower, air-cooled gasoline engine like those used on garden tractors in the States. Dependable and simple to maintain, it consumed only one gallon of fuel an hour. With one drum of gasoline we could travel all the way to Iquitos, 716 miles downriver. The motor lacked reverse and neutral gears and had only a wind-on rope starter, but experienced rivermen assured us these deficiencies would cause no problem once we learned to handle the vessel.

One of those rivermen had been Raúl's helper on the trip from Atalaya. Good-natured and hard-working, José knew the river as far as Iquitos, so we hired him to come along and teach us what he could about handling a small boat on the Amazon.

As the craft neared completion, something about her boxy profile took on a vague familiarity. One afternoon as we applied the last coat of paint—shiny black for the hull, stormy blue for the superstructure—Helen exclaimed, "I know what she looks like. She's even the same size. *African Queen.*"

Five weeks after we found her under the mango tree, our boat moved precariously on rollers to the river's edge, down the bank, and into the water. Riding high and stable, she stood out like a queen in the fleet of drab, unpainted river craft. And so we christened her *Amazon Queen,* breaking a bottle of pisco on her ironshod bow.

A small boy asked me to translate the name into Spanish. When I did he replied, *"Mucho nombre para poco barco.* A lot of name for a little boat." Perhaps, but before we reached Belém, *Amazon Queen* would grow into her name.

Our first morning aboard still stands out vividly in my mind. Deep down in my consciousness, I felt the bunk rock beneath me. I heard the whisper of water, felt the tingle of a breeze still cool from the night. The long pink tongues of Amazonian dawn played across my face, and I remembered where I was. I had not slept so well since we left home. Propping myself on one elbow, I glanced through the screens, still black with mosquitoes trying to get in. José had done a good job of mooring us the previous night. The *Queen* lay with her bow against the shore, tethered to a bamboo pole thrust deep into the mud.

On the other bunk Helen threw an arm across her face to ward off the light, but the yellow bedspread and candy-striped sheets seemed to draw the sun into the white cabin. Balty, confined so long in town, sprawled on the deck between us, still sleeping off the effects of his romp on the sandy beach the

Launching a queen: Workers roll a log into position under the bow of Amazon Queen, *inching the newly completed boat down the riverbank for a trial run. The authors helped to outfit the vessel, built on a 30-foot-long hull of seasoned cedar. Balty dozes on the deck of the compact cabin (bottom) as Frank studies his maps.*

night before. He stirred, stretched, nuzzled Helen and me in turn, and stood at the door. I sprayed away the insects with a bug bomb, let him out, and smiled. At that moment all those weeks of work in Pucallpa's humid heat seemed worth it. At last we were free of the uncertainties of transportation and the daily time-consuming tasks of camping.

"Wake up," I called happily to José in his little wheelhouse-bunkroom, "the day is already half over."

"*Sí,* Señor Frank," he replied from the water under my window, "I have been awake for an hour. I am cleaning the filth off the hull from yesterday."

I had almost forgotten about yesterday. And the day before, and the day before that—the frustrating anguish of hauling *Amazon Queen* into Pucallpa's sewage-scummed backwater to correct its defects. Our mechanic had forgotten to install the packing gland on the rudder post, and we nearly sank in a rush of water on our first trial run. During the second trial, the propeller-shaft bearing heated so badly that we had had to replace it on the spot, groping blindly in the putrid water.

RICHARD SCHLECHT

With the completion of Amazon Queen, *the authors continue down the Ucayali, finally reaching the Amazon proper.*

But on her third time out, *Amazon Queen* far surpassed our expectations. Her tiny motor seemed almost lost in the small engine room, but she proved powerful enough to churn upstream should the need arise, and fast enough to cruise downriver with the current at a comfortable 10 knots. Remarkably stable, she responded nimbly to the wheel. Protected from sun, rain, and insects, well-supplied with canned food, gasoline, and water, we could let whimsy and chance dictate itinerary and schedule. Balty leaped aboard, and we cast off, José poling the bow around into the current while I cranked the engine, its one-cylinder pop-pop almost a profanity on the silent river. Ahead still lay 3,240 miles of the Amazon.

While Helen prepared a breakfast of coffee, scrambled eggs, canned bacon, and toast on the alcohol stove in the galley end of the cabin, I opened the book with which I had read myself to sleep the night before—an 1854 edition of Lt. William Lewis Herndon's *Exploration of the Valley of the Amazon.* Our small ship's library held several books on the subject, all sent ahead to Pucallpa for this phase of the journey. Up to this point, few people had preceded us along our route. But from here on, we would be following in the wake of scientists and explorers, rubber barons, gold seekers, and mutineers, men who had left their mark on an Amazonian history as varied and violent as any in the New World. Herndon, who led a U. S. Navy fact-finding expedition down the river in 1851-52, left his mark in a way no other can claim. He can be credited, at least in part, with giving us *Life on the Mississippi, Huckleberry Finn,* and *Tom Sawyer.* Writing some 50 years after he read Herndon's journal, Mark Twain termed it one of the turning points of his life:

"I was fired with a longing to ascend the Amazon.... At last Circumstance came to my help. It was in this way. Circumstance, to help or hurt another man, made him lose a fifty-dollar bill in the street; and to help or hurt me, made me find it. I advertised the find, and left for the Amazon the same day.... I went by the way of Cincinnati, and down the Ohio and Mississippi. My idea was to take ship, at New Orleans, for Para. In New Orleans I inquired and found there was no ship leaving for Para....

"After a few days I was out of money. Then Circumstance arrived, with another turning-point in my life—a new link. On my way down, I had made the acquaintance of a pilot. I begged him to teach me the river, and he consented. I became a pilot."

Breakfast over, I began my own lessons on how to become a pilot. There was more to learn than I could have imagined. Though it is still called the Ucayali—and would be for another 600 miles until its meeting with the Marañón—this stretch of the Amazon is as complicated as any area along its 4,195-mile course. Perhaps because I had seen its labyrinth of islands and curves from the air, perhaps because no accurate map exists, the river seemed as complex to me as a psychologist's maze. But I felt no "reward" when José saved a whole day's travel along an immense curve by taking a 20-minute short-cut through a tiny natural canal. I wanted to know *how* he chose that canal, how he navigated. I could detect no system, no method.

Why did he hug the banks in some places, almost brushing the branches of great trees where the river had gnawed away at their roots? Why did he steer carefully in the center of the river in other places? Why did he choose narrow channels through tunnels of overhanging trees when a broad expanse of brown river meandered off to one side or the other? How did he know which of the many channels that appeared at every curve would lead on to the "mother" river rather than into the dead-end swamp of a newly cutoff oxbow? Could I ever learn to navigate this constantly changing Amazon?

"You will learn, Señor Frank," José said. "But first you must learn to *read* the river. Everything on the river tells me something. I watch the floating leaves, the logs, the bits of foam. They are in a hurry to reach the sea and will not enter a channel with no outlet. They know the fast current better than I. So I follow them. On the Amazon it is the *fast* water that runs deep."

"And if there is nothing floating, how then do I know the deep water?"

"The river will tell you, Señor. See the ripples ahead. On the Tambo or the Ene that might mean rocks. But below Pucallpa there are no rocks. The ripples are caused by wind fighting the current. Where they are biggest, the current is strongest, and the water deepest. That is where I steer."

"And if there is no wind?"

"Ah, Señor Frank, then I must have trust, for who but God knows where the sandbanks have moved since the last rains. You must learn to trust too. The Amazon is like a woman. You cannot see beneath her skin, but you can know her mood even by what you do not see. It is something you will feel. She has her rules, and you must play by them."

Many of those rules Helen and I would learn by hard experience, but those that José taught us in the days that followed formed the basis of our stormy marriage with the Amazon.

Dwarfed in midstream, Amazon Queen *plows the murky waters of the Ucayali. The river meanders*

716 miles from Pucallpa to Iquitos, more than twice the straight-line distance between the two points.

"Stop!" shouts Helen as her bamboo pole touches a sand bar. Because Amazon Queen *had no fathometer, Helen spent much of the trip probing from the bow. Rain-drenched and mud-spattered, Frank moors to a stake driven into the slippery bank (bottom).*

We learned to spot invisible sand bars by the tranquil water above them, or by the tail of ripples the current formed downstream from half-submerged logs. We learned to choose a channel between steep banks rather than sloping ones, and to cross the river in the deep water downriver from islands rather than over the shallows built up by the current above them.

As José taught us to read the river, so he taught us to handle *Amazon Queen*. We learned to compensate for our lack of reverse gear when making a landing —approaching the shore against the current, throttling back until we barely moved in the water, the bow nudging the bank so gently we hardly felt it touch. We learned to moor the *Queen* with poles rammed in the mud fore and aft so the stern would not swing around into shallow water near the bank. Most of all, we learned to watch the rise and fall of the river as it varied with the rains in the mountains. The Amazon herself taught us that lesson on a black, moonless night about halfway to Iquitos.

We had already adopted the habit of retiring early. The mosquitoes made it an easy habit to get into. From the dusky purple of twilight to the moist yellow dawn, we remained prisoners of swarming black clouds that to me will always make this part of the Amazon an uninhabitable hell.

We had moored even earlier than usual; it had been an unnerving afternoon. In swerving to miss a floating log, *Amazon Queen* had listed sharply, throwing Balty from the deck into the river. Without reverse we could not stop quickly enough. Helpless, we watched him go under the silt-laden water, bob up again, and swim toward us. We came about into the current, but I misjudged its strength and turned too late. Balty swept past, his head going under, his paws churning to keep afloat as the current carried him away from us.

Only his German shepherd intelligence saved him. Seemingly sure that we would come for him, he headed for shore, scrambled up onto the bank, and collapsed. When we finally reached him, he just sat, looking like a small, frightened puppy for all of his 85 pounds.

We moored the *Queen* right there. It was a wild stretch of riverbank with jungle as tangled as a spider's web to the water's edge, as uninviting a place to stop as we had seen. The bank sloped into shallows and we should have known better than to stay, but we were too tense to go on.

Without really seeing or hearing, we watched the reddening sky darken with wave after wave of parrots, wheeling and circling in clouds as dense as locusts, their wings iridescent green jewels in the lowering sun, their raspy cries a harsh din above the still river. With dusk they settled in the trees, and we fell asleep to the garbled murmur of their voices from the forest.

Sometime about midnight Helen shook me awake. Even before she spoke, I knew something was wrong; she seemed to be leaning uphill on the cabin deck. But it was not Helen who was leaning; it was the boat. I played the flashlight through the mosquito-blurred screens. The river had dropped. We were aground and listing badly.

I didn't take time to dress or apply insect repellent. The water was falling too fast. I roused José and together we leaped ashore, waves of mosquitoes homing in on us; they were all over us, in our mouths, eyes, and ears.

We pushed and strained at the bow, but the *Queen* was stuck fast, heeling over more by the minute. I sent Helen and Balty aft inside the cabin, adding

Chinese-born shopkeeper in Requena carefully folds a Peruvian flag his wife sewed for the Schreiders. Amazon Queen flew the flag at her masthead, at the request of the army, until she left Peru. Goods from across the world stock the shelves of the store; in jungle regions the government tries to stimulate trade by lowering import duties.

HELEN AND FRANK SCHREIDER

their weight to the stern in an attempt to lighten the bow. But still the *Queen* wouldn't budge. Helen joined us pushing at the bow, agonizing under a fresh onslaught of mosquitoes, but even the three of us could not move the boat. José suggested we might break her free by rocking the stern in the deeper water there. I splashed into the river, but José stopped me with a shout, beating the water with a stick, stirring up the mud. I had forgotten about the stingrays, eels, and whatever else might be lurking there. But how good the cool water felt to my burning body.

With José and me rocking the stern, Helen pushing on the bow, and with the current etching the mud from under the keel, the *Queen* finally began to slide from the bar where she had settled. We heaved her free into the deeper water offshore. While José held the bow line, Helen and I climbed aboard and started the engine, holding the boat against the current until he could join us. The beam from our searchlight sweeping a white cone across the water, we headed downstream to a deeper mooring. We took turns standing watch all night, our bodies swelling and smarting from the mosquito bites until the antihistamine pills we took did their work.

By morning the river had dropped another foot, enough to have left *Amazon Queen* lying on her side until the next heavy rain in the mountains again raised the level of the water.

Happily, the rest of the 11-day passage to Iquitos proved uneventful by comparison. Each day added to our knowledge of the river, preparing us for the time when we would face it alone. As our knowledge grew so did our confidence, and soon we were instinctively following the line of current along the deep channels. We still could not relax completely, but we spent less time *thinking* about navigating, and more time looking. What had seemed an unchanging panorama of blue sky, green jungle, and brown water became a varied pageant unfolding through our binoculars.

Pink or black porpoises arced with a whoosh of air across our bow, sending Balty into fits of barking. Gaggles of yellow-and-black orioles fluttered on bare-limbed trees fairly dripping with their pouchlike nests. We reveled in the subtle glow of an orchid in the fork of a tree near the water and in the flash of macaws across the sky, their red, yellow, and blue tails streaming behind them like flames.

Cruising for hours past walls of unbroken forest, we sometimes seemed to be the only boat on the river, the only people. Occasionally, the wall opened into lime-green cow pastures dotted with bony grazers. From clumps of thatch shacks that marked tiny villages, tattered children came running to the river to stare. Traffic was indeed sparse on the only surface artery between Pucallpa and Iquitos. A barge-pushing tug passed us one night, its lights shimmering like lightning bugs, its powerful wake rocking us against the mud shore. A raft piled with green bananas bound for Iquitos drifted by. We waved to a few trading boats not much larger than ours. Fishermen in canoes occasionally asked us for aspirin, but that was all. The slow pace of the river seemed to govern the pace of life.

We became well acquainted with the few towns that lay along the last half of our passage. The mosquitoes that had feasted so well the night we went aground did not leave in the morning, and the hundreds that got inside during our frantic maneuvering exhausted the last of our insecticide. Our journey began to follow a script that never varied. The same graying wood shacks, the same bleached thatch roofs and dusty red streets, the same stocks of cane alcohol, cigarettes, and canned beef in the same bare-shelved shops. And the same answer, *"No hay*—There isn't any," to our request for insecticide.

Not until we reached Requena—the "Athens of the Ucayali," a sign over one shop said—did we find relief. And by then the Peruvian Army had added another item to our shopping list. As we chugged slowly into port, a machine gun-toting soldier stopped us. What was that strange flag we were flying? What cargo did we carry? No cargo? Then what *were* we doing on the river? My explanation only made him more suspicious. He took me to his colonel. The colonel ordered *Amazon Queen* searched. Convinced we were not Castroite guerrillas after all, he gave us permission to leave port. But not until we had a Peruvian flag to fly in addition to our National Geographic banner.

Aristotle would have reddened with indignation had he heard the citizens of Requena refer to their hilly city as the Athens of the Ucayali, but by Amazon standards it is certainly a center of learning. Two-thirds of its 5,000 inhabitants are students; fully half come from other areas, deserting the town between sessions. With nine primary schools, four secondary schools, and a teachers' college, Requena offers the only place between Pucallpa and

Iquitos where students can advance beyond the six years of education provided in other villages along the river.

We spent the better part of a day trudging through the city's dusty streets and dustier shops looking for a flag. None was to be had ready-made, and no merchant would rouse himself to make one even though Peru's ensign—a white vertical band flanked by two red ones—is simplicity itself. Materials and sewing machines were prominent in almost every shop, but, with some vague excuse, each proprietor sent us to the next. Finally one shopkeeper referred us to a jovial Chinese who agreed to make the flag while we waited.

By that time Requena's liquid heat had left us with about as much energy as the merchants. We were content to lean against the counter in the full blast of a fan and listen to our benefactor talk of the future of the Amazon. With 40 years' residence in the area, he was in a position to know:

"Right now the Amazon lives on imports. Look at my shelves. Canned food from England, Denmark, the United States, Hong Kong. Textiles from Japan. Tools from Germany. The only reason people can afford such things is because the government tries to stimulate trade in the jungle regions with low import duties. But no matter what is imported, the future depends ultimately on the people. And they just don't like to work."

At the moment I did not find the thought of work in such a climate very attractive either, and I said so.

"But you're not hungry," the Chinese countered. "Around here rice is scarce and expensive. The people just sit around when they could be planting, at least enough for themselves. When the river is low, all they have to do is throw out the seed on the sand bars, wait a while, then harvest it before the river rises. But even that is too much work.

"All these schools here. What do they teach? Mathematics and history. Not one trade school. An education is to use, not sit on. The people need practical knowledge and the desire to use it. They need to take off their shirts and go to work. Then maybe the Amazon will progress.

"Ah, here's your flag," he added as his Peruvian wife came from the back room. In 25 minutes she had produced as fine a flag as I could have asked for.

Any of the other merchants could have done the same. I wondered what a thousand more men as ambitious as this Chinese could accomplish along the Amazon. A few years may answer that question: Japanese immigrants are arriving in Peru from already successful colonies in Brazil. Meanwhile, both Peru and Brazil are becoming increasingly sensitive to the fact that, with few exceptions, foreigners are achieving more in developing the Amazon than their own countrymen. Even here in Requena the distinction was evident: Though the Chinese had taken a Peruvian name, a Peruvian wife, and spoke perfect Spanish, after 40 years he was still called "El Chino."

Two days later *Amazon Queen* lurched across the choppy confluence of the Ucayali and the Marañón. With her Peruvian and National Geographic flags board-stiff in the wind, she bobbed and fishtailed her way through whirlpools and waves greater than anything we had yet seen. Beyond rolled a swift, broad reach of brown water stretching two miles from bank to bank. In the 1,570 miles from its source, the river's name had changed seven times. But from here on the name would change no more. We had reached the Amazon.

Ucayali waypoints: Riverbank footpaths lead toward the tiny settlement of Alto Perillo; curious children flock around Helen at Flor de Punga. In many such villages the Schreiders found squat, metal-roofed houses replacing traditional thatch homes.

Postscripts to History: *A City, a Village,*

CHAPTER SIX

OLD-TIMERS along the Amazon still speak of the "great rubber boom." The Indian remembers it with horror, the white with nostalgia, and the *mestizo* with emotions as mixed as his European-Indian lineage. The 25-year period from 1890 to 1915 produced an orgy of opulence and a frenzy of fear and madness virtually unparalleled in the history of the New World. In area of exploitation and number of people involved, if not in product value, the rubber boom exceeded even the gold rushes to California, Alaska, and the Yukon Territory. It brought death to thousands, slavery to more thousands, and fantastic wealth to hundreds. Almost every town on the Amazon bears the boom's beauty marks and scars, its palaces and hovels. When it was over, the Amazon went back to sleep, but for a while the river was lustily alive.

Legend has it that Columbus observed Indians playing ball in Haiti on his second voyage to the Americas, but no definitive description of rubber's properties reached Europe until the French scientist Charles Marie de la Condamine descended the Amazon in 1743. Fascinated by the milky latex that oozed from the bark of *Hevea brasiliensis,* the wild rubber tree, La Condamine reported that the Indians made waterproof jars by pouring the thick, white liquid over a mud mold, smoking it over a fire, then breaking the mold and extracting the pieces. He described how Portuguese settlers made boots and bottles from rubber. They waterproofed cloth with it too, though 88 years passed before a man named Macintosh manufactured the first raincoat.

In the meantime British chemist Joseph Priestley observed that a blob of India rubber removed pencil marks. Shoes made of raw rubber that yellowed with age — advertised as "golden slippers" — became the fashion in the United States. But people did not like their shoes becoming sticky in summer and stiff in winter, as always happened with anything made of untreated rubber, and the fad passed. Working independently, Charles Goodyear of the United States and Thomas Hancock of England discovered that cooking raw rubber with sulphur made it pliable and soft all year round. Hancock described the process as being similar to the bubbling of lava in a volcano, with a smell as vile, and a new word — vulcanization — entered the lexicon of science. When Scotsman John Dunlop developed the pneumatic tire in 1888, he did more than smooth

In smoky discomfort, an Indian tapper cures a ball of wild latex on a spit. Beginning in 1890, a clamor for rubber brought a quarter-century heyday of prosperity to the Amazon, but the boom soon waned as Asian plantations came into full production.

and Two Visions of Jungle Riches

HELEN AND FRANK SCHREIDER

Framed by scales from another era, warehousemen in Manaus, Brazil, split open balls of unprocessed rubber to inspect them for stones, twigs, and trash, and to grade them according to quality. A 50-pound ball may bring $15. Opposite, a rubber tree, Hevea brasiliensis, gradually bleeds a large cupful of latex. Tappers cut into the bark to release the sticky sap. Stevedores (lower left) unload the heavy balls, collected along the Amazon and its many tributaries. Widely scattered trees make tapping difficult and inefficient; Brazil imports more than 50 percent of its natural rubber.

the ride of the world's bicycles and automobiles; he also stirred up a storm along the Amazon.

European and American manufacturers clamored for more and more rubber. Amazonians could sell all they produced. The price kept rising, reaching $2.90 a pound, and rubber became big business.

People still speak of the *patrón* who "owned" millions of acres of land and everything on it. Title was rarely established, but in the days of the boom no one cared. The patrón staked out his claim, often to a whole river, and recruited his own army to guard it. He hired a motley crew of rubber tappers and kept them supplied with canned food, rice, clothes, machetes, and mosquito nets on credit. The tapper paid in rubber, but he soon learned that the only ones making a fortune were the patrones and their agents, the "rubber barons" of the Amazonian port cities of Iquitos, Manaus, and Belém.

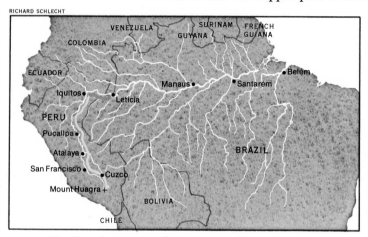

Heading downstream from Iquitos, the authors encounter a river so wide that haze blurs trees along the far bank.

He learned too that tapping rubber was hard, miserable work. There were no plantations; the trees grew wild, often in areas miles apart. Ravaged by malaria and poor nutrition, subject to tuberculosis from perpetual dampness, the tapper spent months at a time in the jungle slicing the bark of the trees, mounting his cups, collecting the latex, smoking it over wood fires, and then carrying the huge black lumps on his back to a collection center. Overcharged for his supplies, underpaid for his rubber, ignorant of accounts if any were kept, the tapper became an indentured worker at best, a maltreated slave at worst.

He could be transferred with his debt and without his agreement from one patrón to the next. He could not even run away; no other patrón would take him, and if he managed to reach a town the police there sent him back. But they could not stop him from talking. Word spread of conditions in the rubber camps; new recruits became scarce, while the demand for rubber increased. To fill the gap, the patrón turned to the Indian.

Peru, Colombia, and Brazil had had Indian antislavery laws for centuries. For just as long they had been ignored. Who was going to enforce the laws when everyone from government officials on down profited from the Indians' labor? Catholic priests who tried to protect the Indians often were expelled from the area. White and mestizo patrones lorded over the Indians with guns and clubs by day and penned them like animals at night. The patrón demanded a quota, and when the tapper failed to meet it he was punished. Along at least one Amazon tributary he was beaten for the first failure, lost an ear for the second, another ear for the third, and was killed for the fourth. Conditions grew so bad that international commissions were set up to investigate.

The world listened in horrified astonishment as the atrocities along Peru's Putumayo River were exposed — floggings, torture, and murders, slave-breeding camps, patrón-sired boys raised to be whip-wielding guards. But despite a call for a boycott on Amazonian latex, people went right on buying until cheaper rubber from Asia ended the boom. One "baron" finally stood trial for his crimes. He came from Iquitos, the early 20th-century rubber center of the Peruvian Amazon, a hundred twisting miles below the confluence of the Ucayali and the Marañón.

Visiting Iquitos in 1851, Lieutenant Herndon had found a tiny fishing village with 227 inhabitants. Cotton and coffee trees grew untended in the dirt streets. Six decades later the village had blossomed into a thriving city of 15,000 residents—and even more transients. In the cool of evening, fashionable ladies in pinch-waisted long gowns strolled the *Malecón*, the colonnaded promenade along the river. Men in white linen suits discussed the price of rubber in the lounge of the Malecón Palace, a luxury hotel brilliantly faced with glazed colored tile from Portugal. An iron building prefabricated in Paris by Alexandre Gustave Eiffel of tower fame housed the exclusive Clube Social Iquitos. At weekly balls, musicales, and dramas, Paris fashions and French champagne dominated the evening. British vessels of the Booth Line provided monthly service from Liverpool. Iquitos, 2,500 miles up the Amazon, had become an international port.

It was easy for Helen and me to imagine Iquitos as the rubber barons knew the city. The old iron bandstand with its stained-glass cornice, the bronze statues in the neatly trimmed plazas, the Spanish- and Portuguese-tile fronts of shops and homes, all speak wistfully of those booming days, now long past.

Booth Line ships still call, tying up at the rusty floating dock that rises and falls as much as 35 feet with the seasonal fluctuations of the river. But they arrive almost empty and leave the same way. A few old men play cards on the frayed green-baize tables in the Clube Iquitos, but the social splendor is gone. Lovers stroll the Malecón, but they now dodge barricades where the river has eaten away the earth beneath crumbling cement. And the Malecón Palace has become a military headquarters.

One thing has not changed, however. The city still plays host to an international cast of characters in the drama of man against the jungle. If you don't find them in the air-conditioned lounge of the Hotel Turista, try Zorba's, the Greek bar around the corner, or the Caravelle, the French-run sidewalk cafe just off the Malecón. The Belgian manager of the Hotel Imperial Amazonas is a fount of information; Marge Smith, American manager of Explorama Tours, arranges blowgun contests between Yagua Indians and plies guests with gourmet dinners in her jungle camp; and a Chinese named Wong can arrange anything from a fishing expedition to an alligator shoot. Chasing down various leads, within two days we met an American chicle buyer, a British shipping manager, a Swiss exporter of tropical fish, two American artists making exotic jewelry from beetle wings and fish eyes, and several other Americans doing research in tropical medicine. By the time we left, we also had become acquainted with an international commune of hippies who were growing marijuana on a houseraft and experimenting with hallucinatory jungle drugs in the floating village of Belén, Iquitos's small-boat port.

Iquitos collects more than characters. It also supplies a large percentage of the tropical fish in home aquariums around the world, squirrel monkeys used

Farthest inland of any world port, Iquitos, Peru, crowds the bank of the Amazon 2,500 miles upstream from its mouth. The city crowns a bluff overlooking the river (above), but each year floods of 30 to 35 feet sweep away more and more of the waterfront. Iquitos throbbed with excitement during the rubber boom, mushrooming from a tiny jungle village to a community of 15,000. Today tourists, wild-animal exports, and jungle-oriented industries nourish the port's economy. A narrow walkway (left) links the bustling city with its floating neighbor Belén (opposite, right).

in medical research, and the jaguars, tapirs, snakes, and birds displayed in many zoos. The animal- and fish-export business has become so large that a special airline was organized to handle the traffic. Nicknamed the Flying Zoo, Copisa Airlines makes weekly flights directly to Miami.

Cooling off at the Caravelle one evening after watching the loading of a cargo of crated animals and fish in oxygen-charged plastic bags aboard a Copisa Lockheed Constellation, we struck up a conversation with Patrick Nicholls, the drolly British Booth Line resident manager. An authority on Amazon commerce, Pat is also an avid amateur entomologist.

"I'm just on my way home," Pat said. "Have to feed Charlie here." He patted a squirming bulge inside his shirt, and a kitten-size monkey peeped out, blinked its large round eyes, and scooted back under cover. "Nocturnal. Doesn't like light. Come along to the chalet, and I'll show you my bugs."

Built half a century ago from material left over from the construction of the floating dock, the Chalet Booth—as the line's large, white residence is called—lies near the edge of town in a huge garden. On the way I queried Pat about the commercial future of Iquitos.

"Depressing," he replied, as he wheeled his Land-Rover along the wide paved streets, past shops, ice-cream parlors, and movie theaters, and then through the small, new residential area with its neat concrete and wood-paneled homes. "We all thought Iquitos would come back to life in 1964 when the government offered a 15-year tax holiday for new businesses here. Dozens of shops opened to sell luxury goods. Peruvian tourists came from all over the country to shop.

"We even brought frozen chickens in from the States. Sold them for less than the local fowl. It's still cheaper to ship goods here from Europe than from Lima. But then the government put an embargo on most imports and a tax on exports. Now Iquitos is dying again."

As we drove through the garden, Pat's handyman closed the gates behind us and hurried off down the street.

"Can't keep servants here after dark," Pat complained. "They keep hearing noises. I tell them it's just this old iron house creaking when it cools off. But then they ask me about the billiard table and the balls that keep clacking when no one is playing."

Pat headed toward a pen at one side of the garden. "I'll just feed Charlie the deer over here. You go on in. If you see an old gentleman in a rocking chair on the porch—he'll be wearing a white suit and black bow tie—just walk right through him."

Helen and I digested that comment and decided to feed Charlie too. The doe licked Pat's hand affectionately, as did the two dogs that came bounding up. I asked their names, already suspecting what the answer would be.

"Both Charlie," Pat replied. "All my animals are named Charlie. Less confusing that way." He looked around. "Charlie the anaconda should be about somewhere. Lives under the house, all 20 feet of him. Can't imagine where he is. Always used to come out and greet my guests. I miss him."

Workman tugs two large caiman hides along a loading platform at a factory on the Amazon. The firm processes thousands of the reptiles for shoes, belts, and purses. Professional hunters have nearly exterminated caimans in some areas along the river.

NATIONAL GEOGRAPHIC PHOTOGRAPHER GEORGE F. MOBLEY (LOWER), AND LOREN McINTYRE

Unlocking the jungle's potential: Forest-crunching behemoth can clear a path 4 miles long and 26 feet wide in an hour. Booms topple trees as tall as 150 feet, and knife-bladed rollers chop them up. This cleared acreage, a pepper farm in eastern Peru, went from jungle to harvest in less than a year. Other land in this area will yield rice and livestock pasture. Axman (left) works as a lumberjack out of Iquitos. In a plywood factory (upper left) a hoist lifts mahogany logs toward a cutting machine.

Objects of Amazon Indian art surround Edith and Jay Louthian in their Iquitos gallery. Indian paddles, masks, and a ceremonial bark-cloth shield hang on the walls. An appliquéd Shipibo skirt at her side, Edith sorts jewelry she has made from such jungle materials as dyed animal bones and teeth, fish and caiman scales, and seed pods. In early 1969, after four years in Iquitos, the Louthians moved their shop to New York City in search of a larger market. At right, Patrick Nicholls, Booth Line manager in Iquitos, nuzzles Charlie, a douroucouli, or night monkey.

We didn't, and we were just as happy to find no old gentleman on the porch.

"I've never seen him myself," Pat confessed as we sat in the high-ceilinged bar, "but a Booth Line captain I know swears *he* has. Stone sober too. From his description it could only be old Massey's ghost. Massey was Booth Line manager here for 40 years. He loved his billiards. Shipped his own table over from England.

"I have heard the billiard balls though. Many's the night I've gotten up to check, but never a soul around.

"I've often wondered if that wasn't what drove old Charlie over there to drink. Died of it, poor chap."

Pat gestured toward a corner. A stuffed monkey sat on a shelf with his arms wrapped around a bottle. By then we had begun to wonder whether some of our host's tales weren't taller than the jungle he had chosen to live in. But in one area Pat didn't need to stretch the truth. His collection of insects ranked as the finest we had ever seen outside a museum.

Pat showed us tray after tray of finely mounted specimens, each more staggering than the last. We marveled at saucer-size butterflies as blue as an electric spark, horned beetles nearly as big as Helen's fist, ants as long as my little finger, hairy-legged tarantulas 7 inches across, a brown moth camouflaged with the mask of an owl's face on its wings. With creatures like these, Helen and I thought, was it any wonder that the Amazon encourages exaggeration?

Amazon Queen's throbbing deck felt good beneath our feet as we took to the river once more, this time without José's practiced hand at the wheel. Near the mouth of the Napo River below Iquitos, we stopped at the village of Francisco de Orellana, named in honor of the Spanish conquistador who became the first European to descend the Amazon.

There, in the middle of a grassy field where children play soccer, a 60-foot-tall brick-and-concrete pylon spears skyward, commemorating the February day in 1542 when Orellana and his companions sailed from the Napo onto the mighty river for which they knew no name. Six months later the beleaguered band of adventurers reached the Atlantic, completing the first known crossing of the South American continent.

Aboard the Peruvian Navy gunboat Marañón, *young people of Iquitos cruise the Amazon. The ship's doctor and two guests strum guitars and sing for the group. At lower right, the* Marañón *sails on civic action duty, delivering construction equipment and school supplies, repairing motors and generators, and offering medical aid to people in remote areas along the river. Below, armed rangers patrol near Iquitos.*

Paddling from the bow, an Indian ferries his family across the Amazon in a pelting rain. Iquitos averages 103 inches of rainfall a year; except in two brief dry seasons, showers occur almost daily. Even in August, the driest month, 5 inches usually falls.

HELEN AND FRANK SCHREIDER

The chronicle of the journey, recorded by Gaspar de Carvajal, a Dominican friar who accompanied the expedition, is filled with tales of gleaming white cities, of "royal highways" built of stone, of white Indians "taller by a span" than the Spaniards, of the finest porcelain "that has ever been seen in the world, for that of Málaga is not its equal," and of fair female warriors where none has been found since. Historians have come to discredit much of the richly storied journal; but fact or fiction, Carvajal's account of battling warrior women who fought "as ten Indian men" has lived on to give the Amazon the name we know it by today.

Judging from the sketchy biographical details available, Orellana appears to have stood a cut above most of the other conquistadors. Unlike his comrades-in-arms, he tried to win the friendship of the Indians and learn their language, resorting to battle only when necessary. But when he did fight, he fought well. He served valiantly in the Inca wars, losing an eye and winning the sobriquet One-Eyed Knight. When Gonzalo Pizarro, half-brother of Peru's conqueror, Francisco Pizarro, announced an expedition to search for the fabled El Dorado and La Canela, Orellana volunteered his services, personal fortune, and all the men he could muster.

La Canela, the Land of Cinnamon, was alluring enough. Orellana well knew how popular the spice had become with the court in Spain; anyone finding a good supply of cinnamon was sure to find favor with the King as well.

But El Dorado remained the ultimate goal. Like every other Spaniard, Orellana had dreamed of that wondrous land, so rich in gold that each new ruler was anointed with resinous gums and then powdered with the precious metal until his body literally gleamed. Tales of El Dorado had been trickling out of the jungle ever since the Indians had learned that the surest way to avoid being burned alive or torn apart by savage dogs was to tell the rapacious Spaniards what they wanted to hear—that there were even richer lands farther to the east, the farther the better.

The army Gonzalo Pizarro led in search of El Dorado and La Canela was as impressive as the continent had yet seen. Where Francisco Pizarro had conquered all of the Inca Empire with only 106 infantry and 62 horsemen, Gonzalo set off with 220 mounted soldiers, 4,000 Indian slaves, 2,000 hogs, almost as many fighting dogs, and an unrecorded number of llamas to carry his supplies. Sixteen months later he stumbled back into Quito, his clothes rotting on his back.

Of his once-valiant army, only 80 emaciated Spaniards remained. Gone were his horses, Indians, hogs, dogs, and llamas. The Amazon jungle had defeated the doughty Gonzalo. For this he blamed Orellana—the man he had trusted to forage ahead for food had disappeared.

But the jungle did not defeat the One-Eyed Knight. Soon after Gonzalo returned to Quito he learned that Orellana had not only survived, but that he also had discovered and navigated the Amazon, claimed it for the King of Spain, and been made governor of all of Amazonas. To Gonzalo it must have seemed bitter irony that such reward should come to the man he was even then charging with treason and desertion.

Experts are still debating the events leading up to those charges. Pizarro, after wandering about for almost ten months through the mountainous jungles of eastern Ecuador, had discovered what Amazon lumbermen today realize all too well: Unlike birds, trees of a kind are seldom found together. He had located cinnamon, but the trees were too scattered to be of much value. Weakened with hunger, the Spaniards pushed on through increasingly difficult terrain, so difficult that when they reached a large river, a tributary of the Napo, Pizarro ordered a boat built to carry their supplies and injured. By the time it was finished, all the dogs, hogs, and llamas had been eaten. Only a few horses remained. All the Indians had died or deserted. When Orellana volunteered to scout ahead for food, promising to return in 12 days, Pizarro agreed. Orellana took the boat and 15 commandeered canoes and headed downriver with 59 men, including Friar Carvajal.

Up to this point the story is relatively clear, and most historians agree in essence if not in detail. But from here on we must rely on the good friar's chronicle: "...we promptly started off...with very great haste....We journeyed on for three days without [finding] any inhabited country at all. Seeing that we had come far...and that we had used up what little food we had... the Captain and the companions conferred...although we did wish to go back up the river, that was not possible on account of the heavy current...and so ...it was decided that we should...go forward and follow the river, [and thus] either die or see what there was along it, trusting in Our Lord...to preserve our lives until we should see our way out...." *(Continued on page 135)*

Broad Napo River snakes through northeastern Ecuador. Francisco de Orellana, first European to descend

the Amazon, sailed down the Napo, reaching the great river in 1542, then pushing on to its mouth.

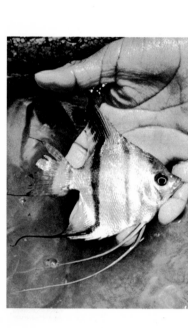

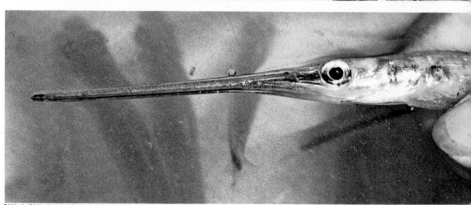

PAUL A. ZAHL, N.G.S. STAFF (UPPER RIGHT), AND LOREN McINTYRE

Razor-toothed piranha, a species of Serrasalmus, *surfaces amid floating Salvinia ferns (opposite). Frenzied by the smell of blood, a school of piranhas can strip a 100-pound animal to its skeleton in a minute. Collectors search the Amazon for exotic specimens of its more than 2,000 fish species; the common angelfish,* Pterophyllum scalare, *at far left thrives in home aquariums. Sharply elongated jaws belong to a freshwater needlefish,* Potamoraphis guianensis. *The peaceful behavior of the inch-long tetras,* Moenkhausia oligolepis *(below), belies their relationship to the piranha. A young girl stretches out atop a giant* Victoria regia *water lily (bottom); growing to 6 feet in diameter, the pads often cover miles of shallow Amazon backwater.*

Young Yagua Indian reacts in a universal manner to a spoonful of medicine admin- istered by Mike Tsalickis, a professional hunter and dealer in wild animals who has befriended the Yaguas. A one-man conglomerate based in Leticia, Colombia, Tsalickis manages a hotel and owns a luxury lodge, a guide service, a brick factory, and an ice plant. The Yaguas who live near Leticia have become accustomed to boat-borne tourists visiting their jungle villages and readily provide blowgun demonstrations.

JAMES R. HOLLAND

Four centuries later Helen and I sweated in the shade of man's frail monument to Orellana. Erected in 1942 on the fourth centennial of his voyage, it already was being reclaimed by the jungle. Spiny grass crumbled the mortar between bricks, and roots split the cement facing. Weathered away by sun, wind, and rain, the words were barely legible. There, beneath the eroded brick prow that represented Orellana's boat, the enormity of what we were attempting struck home as it never had before.

Many things had changed along the Amazon, but the river remained a formidable adversary. The expanse of sepia water was already so wide that the trees on the far bank were blurred by haze. I recalled a conversation with the American chicle buyer in Iquitos, a veteran of eight years on the Amazon.

"I'm not saying you can't make it," he had told us, "but anyone who knows this river knows what you are challenging. Never underestimate it or the harsh land it flows through. Never relax."

Underestimate the Amazon? Unlikely. Relax? Impossible. Just getting under way in the morning set up a tension that lasted all day. With no reverse and no neutral, timing was crucial. While Helen poled at the stern to keep the current from swinging us into shore, I pushed off at the bow, scrambled aboard, set the wheel, and raced aft to the engine room, often bumping into Helen as she hurried forward to hold the bow away from the bank with another pole. When she signaled that all was clear ahead, I yanked on the starter rope. It was at times like these that we missed José most. He had known the precise angle to point the bow so that the current would carry us into the channel instead of back toward shore, and the exact moment to start the engine. Weeks passed before we developed that finely tuned sense of timing needed to swing into the channel before the current carried us into propeller-fouling reeds, a submerged log, or a sand bar.

Once we got under way, however, José's teaching paid off. Though we were still using aerial charts for navigation, though hidden sand bars kept Helen on the bow probing the depths with a pole, I began to detect subtle changes in the rumble of the propeller when we approached shallows. As the days passed we felt more at ease when we crossed and recrossed the river following the deep outside curves. But we never lost the feeling of insignificance in this green and brown world that so quickly subjects man to the perspective of nature. Herndon's description of the Amazon, put on paper more than a century earlier, seemed to echo in our ears:

"The march of the great river in its silent grandeur was sublime; but in the untamed might of its turbid waters, as they cut away its banks, tore down the gigantic denizens of the forest, and built up islands, it was awful. . . . Its waters looked angry, sullen, and relentless; and the whole scene awoke emotions of awe and dread."

Herndon's frustrated exclamation, "This river seems interminable!" became our own. The long days and empty, closed jungle passed so slowly. We looked forward to the quiet hours between dusk and dawn when the uneven song of the forest replaced the steady hum of the motor. But finding a place to spend those quiet hours often proved as trying as getting under way. The river was still going down, and after our experience on the Ucayali we looked for steep banks where we saw canoes tied up. Small-boat traffic was sparse, and our arrival always brought a flood of ragged children and packs of small, yapping dogs from the grass huts set back from the bank.

Invariably we were taken for a pair of itinerant merchants; the people could never understand that we traveled for reasons other than commerce, that we had no rice to sell, no sugar, no salt, matches, or cigarettes. Most often they asked for medicines, and we shared our small stock of aspirin and anti-malarial pills. When we refused payment they insisted we accept an egg or two, a papaya, a hand of bananas, or a pineapple. Almost always we felt welcome at these moorings. This was hardly the case, however, as we tied up one evening in the "land of the three frontiers," where Peru, Brazil, and Colombia join. The man who ran to meet us didn't ask what we had to sell, only what we were carrying. When we told him we were just travelers he advised us to find another mooring downstream. I replied that it had been a trying day, that we had gone aground four times and had lost the channel twice in a maze of islands, that this mooring seemed fine. He shrugged and walked away.

We ate and turned in early. Sometime later Helen woke me with a sleepy cry, "Frank. The stars are moving." Then, more startled, "No, it's not the stars. We're adrift. We're in the middle of the river."

For the inexperienced, navigating the Amazon by day is awesome. By night it is terrifying. We had no idea how long we had been drifting nor how we had slipped our mooring. We could not tell where we were. I hauled in the ropes that trailed in the water, started the engine, and headed slowly for the closer bank. A hundred, perhaps two hundred yards from shore, I couldn't tell, we ran aground. I reached for a pole to shove off—we kept them on the roof when we were traveling—but they weren't there.

I remembered that I had stuck them in the mud for mooring posts. But if they had just pulled out of the mud, letting us drift off, I would have found them when I pulled in the ropes. At least I would have found the knotted loops if the poles had slipped through. But there had been no poles and no knots. We had been deliberately untied and pushed off into the current.

Beating the black water with my cupped palms, I jumped overboard, pushed the boat free, and scrambled back on deck. Helen spotted a faint glow on the far bank, and we headed for it, blessing the Amazonians' fear of the night that causes them to leave candles or lanterns burning in their doorways. It was a miserable mooring in a patch of mosquito-clouded reeds, but it was deep.

Neither of us could sleep. We stood watch all night, wondering aloud how even a stealthy jungle dweller could have untied our mooring and pushed us off without waking Balty. Even more we wondered why.

Later we related the story to an old river hand. "This is smugglers' country," he explained. "Biggest business on the river. Gold, diamonds, cigarettes, liquor—they carry anything. That chap might even have thought you were one of them. Otherwise, why did he ask what you were carrying? He was expecting someone, that's for sure, and you came along at the wrong time. He had to get rid of you. You were lucky he didn't do more than just set you adrift."

Blowgun-wielding Yagua dons the palm-fiber headdress of his ancestors. Such flowing tresses may have led Orellana to mistake attacking Indians for women—thus giving the river its name. Historians today discredit Orellana's stories of female warriors.

Monkeys, Manatees, and Mirages: In the

CHAPTER SEVEN

NLESS YOU'RE LOOKING FOR LETICIA or see a ship tied up there, you easily could pass it by. And that would be a shame. Not that Leticia itself is so much, but you'd miss a chance to meet one of the great characters of the Amazon. Prior to the mid-1950's this little port—Colombia's only access to the Amazon—rarely showed on maps. Mike Tsalickis put it there; when he moved in, things began to happen.

Wiry, dynamic Mike, a Greek-American from Tarpon Springs, Florida, is the kind of man who makes things move. Anyone who tries to keep up with Mike has to move too—and fast. By the time we located him, we had traipsed from his office to his animal-collecting center, to his new luxury lodge, to the older hotel he manages, to his brick factory, ice plant, Booth Line agency, the hospital and cable office he persuaded the Colombian Government to install, and finally to the new airport where he was meeting one of the scheduled flights from Bogotá that he had talked Avianca Airlines into initiating. The planes not only take out Mike's animals, but they also bring in increasing numbers of tourists. To make sure they are well taken care of, the attractive new air terminal offers the facilities of a guide service. Mike runs that too.

"There's been a lot of criticism of animal trappers lately," Mike commented as he led us past large, spotless, tiled cages squirming with snakes, fluttering with parrots and macaws, scurrying with monkeys. He stopped to soothe a frightened little jaguar cub that had just been brought in and ordered a helper to change the water in a tub of turtles. We couldn't help comparing aloud the condition of Mike's animals with those we had observed in Peruvian trapping centers in Iquitos. We had seen some 300 monkeys jammed into a pen the size of a refrigerator, ocelot kittens panting in the heat without water, a cageful of macaws so crowded that the birds could neither stretch their necks nor spread their wings.

"That's what I mean," Mike went on. "Unless animal trappers improve the conditions, humane societies in the United States and Europe are going to force us all out of business—even those of us who treat our animals well. In addition to providing animals for zoos, we also ship hundreds of squirrel monkeys to medical research laboratories every month. That's another problem. Conservationists say that soon there won't be any monkeys left. I don't believe that.

Colorfully camouflaged, a 4-foot green tree snake, Leptophis ahaetulla, *slithers along a branch. It shares the warm, moist climate of the Amazon Basin with some 100 other snake species, including the venomous bushmaster and the dreaded fer-de-lance.*

Wake of the One-Eyed Knight

HELEN AND FRANK SCHREIDER

Cradling a long-snouted freshwater dolphin, Inia geoffrensis, *hunter Mike Tsalickis cautiously lifts the sleek mammal from a Peruvian creek; a visiting Japanese zoologist waits to hand up another. A dealer in animals of the Amazon since 1953, the Greek-American from Tarpon Springs, Florida, employs hundreds of hunters along the river. Squirrel monkeys,* Saimiri sciureus *(left), their long tails helping them keep their balance, will stock scientific laboratories and medical schools in the United States. The fluffy fur of a saki monkey,* Pithecia monachus *(below left), makes it look several times its 3 to 4 pounds. Tsalickis's assistants work through the night to crate a shipment of squirrel monkeys at his animal compound in Leticia, Colombia.*

Trappers haven't even touched the jungle back from the rivers yet. But just to make sure there's a good supply, I bought an island upriver. Stocked it with squirrel monkeys and planted it with bananas and papayas, both fruits that the animals like. They're free there to lead a normal life until we need them."

The three of us strolled over to a row of large, round, concrete tubs. In the bottom of one a dozen or so snakelike creatures 5 to 6 feet long slithered about in 6 inches of water. One of Mike's assistants fended them off with a pole while he cleaned the basin.

"Electric eels," Mike said. "Each one can make a neon light glow or knock a man unconscious, even kill him if he has a weak heart. These will go to a laboratory in the States that is doing enzyme research in the treatment of mental illness. We shipped 1,000 eels last year, and the lab wants 6,000 more. High water makes trapping difficult. I hope we'll be able to catch that many."

"I hope so too," I echoed, thinking of how many times I had wondered if there were any eels around when I jumped into the river to push *Amazon Queen* off a sand bar.

"What's this over here?" Helen asked, pointing to a tub filled with agitated water hyacinths.

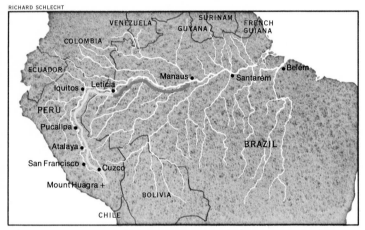

Taking to the river again after a brief stop in Leticia, the authors cross into Brazil, bound for historic Manaus.

"A manatee, or sea cow," Mike answered. "They're getting scarce on the Amazon. Indians eat them. There used to be lots of them in Florida. They fed on water hyacinth. Kept it under control. But they were hunted almost out of existence, and the water hyacinth took over many of Florida's lakes. We're trying to repopulate up there by shipping in manatees."

I had never seen a manatee, but I knew that they are mammals with broad, flat tails, and that the female has teats and suckles her young. Somewhere I had read that because of these characteristics early Spanish explorers had mistaken manatees for mermaids. When I asked Mike what he thought about this, he grinned.

"We're going to change the water in a few minutes. After you've had a good look at this lady here, you tell me."

Helen and I leaned over the edge of the tub as the men scooped away the hyacinth and drained the water. A swish of shiny gray skin appeared, then a tail, and finally a whiskery, round face with miniscule, black, marblelike eyes. Such a face not even a companionship-starved explorer could love.

Mike's tenderness with animals and his easy grace under the pressures of his many business interests belied the tenor of television shows and magazine articles that presented him only as a fearless jungle trapper. I asked whether he still lassoed caimans and wrestled snakes.

"Sure thing," he replied. "That's fun. One of my men reported a big anaconda not far from here. Why not come along when I go after him tomorrow?"

Early next morning, with Mike and four of his helpers, we sped in a motor-boat along a narrow, winding creek leading from the Amazon into a large black-water lake. *Victoria regia* lily pads, growing to six feet in diameter, clustered like coasters near the shore. An Indian cast a net for small fish while another stood poised in a canoe to harpoon a giant *paiche,* one of the aquatic marvels of the Amazon. Weighing up to 300 pounds, the paiche's scales make fine fingernail files. Its tongue, when dried, is so rough and hard the Indians use it for a wood rasp. And its flesh makes the tastiest fish steaks I have ever eaten.

Across the lake we entered another creek, much narrower than the first and overhung with trees. Mike signaled the motorman to slow down.

"Anacondas, or water boas, are good swimmers," he said softly. "Don't often catch them in water. Have to find them in the trees. But they're hard to see."

After that Helen and I saw water boas on every limb. But Mike didn't.

"Too bad," he said. "I'm glad I brought one along to show you how it's done."

"One what?" Helen asked, looking around the boat.

"Why a water boa," Mike answered. "Just a small one, 15 feet or so," Mike nudged a burlap bag near my wife's feet. It began to squirm. Helen, who had faced a charging rhino in Africa, frightened away a grizzly in Alaska, and tracked Bengal tigers in India, nearly upset the boat in her flight from boa to stern.

The motorman swung the boat toward a clearing in the jungle, and Mike dragged the burlap bag onto the bank. "Anacondas eat only every week or two," Mike remarked, opening the bag. "This one's still digesting his last meal, so I'm afraid he'll be a bit sluggish."

"Don't apologize," Helen said, climbing onto a fallen tree trunk.

A hundred-pound snake, 15 feet long and almost 8 inches thick, is impressive enough behind an iron grill. Crawling freely a few yards away from you, he's spectacular. We watched his great flat head emerge from the bag. His tongue flicked out like a lancet, and he uncoiled—like one great rippling muscle taut as a cable under his mottled gold-and-black skin.

If a snake can be beautiful, this one certainly was. He radiated raw power. He belonged in the jungle, not in a zoo. When he headed for the water, I couldn't help but wish that he would get away. But Mike and his helpers were ready. They headed him off, and he turned back up the bank toward the tree where Helen was standing. Bewildered, not knowing which way to turn, the anaconda coiled under the trunk. I believe now that a snake can hypnotize. Fascinated in spite of her fear, Helen leaned over for a better look. Startled, the snake headed for the water again, much faster than I would have thought, and much faster than Mike had anticipated. His men grabbed the snake's tail, Mike grabbed its head, and the creature arched its thick coils toward the tree trunk.

Helen moved even faster. Her feet slipped on the slick bark, and she fell toward the snake, twisted in midair, executed a perfect in-flight course correction, and plopped to the ground on the far side of the log. By the time she had picked herself up, the snake was back in the bag.

Helen had been in no real danger—Mike had wrestled larger snakes by himself. "You know," he said when he had stopped laughing, "I've worked with a lot of photographers, but I've never seen one go into orbit before—nor make such a graceful, soft landing."

"Who said it was soft?" Helen countered, ruefully rubbing her backside.

Richly varied, Amazonia's feathered vertebrates number more than 1,000 species. At his island home near Macapá, Brazil, retired Dutch diplomat Pieter van Scherpenberg shows off two pet parrots — a scarlet macaw, Ara macao, *on his arm and a golden conure,* Aratinga guarouba. *A disklike crest crowns the brilliantly plumed male cock-of-the-rock,* Rupicola peruviana *(below left). The young spectacled owl,* Pulsatrix perspicillata *(below right), will change color when it matures — its belly turning buff and its head and breast black, with white rims encircling the patches around its eyes. The double-crested harpy eagle,* Harpia harpyja *(bottom left), preys on sloths, monkeys, and other birds. Lice eggs dot the blue skin of an adult hoatzin,* Opisthocomus hoazin, *a bird that climbs well but flies poorly.*

Most days Leticia remains a quiet little Amazonian town. But one morning shortly before we left, it suddenly came alive. The M.V. *Cyril,* one of the larger Booth Line ships, had arrived during the night, and in a flurry of activity, the gray, wooden warehouses that front the river disgorged the jungle products they had been hoarding.

The stench of rotting flesh poured with almost physical force from dark doorways where men hurried to salt down slimy caiman skins. Dried wild pig hides, bristly and stiff as boards, lay stacked in bales on the dock. Cigarettes, canned fruit, and case after case of canned sardines came from *Cyril*'s hold. That was about all, however; the 2,300-ton ship was traveling almost empty. I wondered how long Booth Line could maintain her service.

"Oh, we'll hang on," the captain told us. "Business is bound to pick up. It always has before. We've been running a service on the Amazon too long to pull out just because things are a little slow right now."

Capt. Philip Baxter welcomed us aboard with a grin that creased the sun wrinkles at the corners of his startlingly blue eyes. Sideburns bristled on cheeks bronzed by 12 years on the Amazon.

"In the old days we said that when you made captain you were filling a dead man's shoes. That's how popular the Amazon run was—a captain didn't retire until he died. Before my time, of course. During the rubber boom. Ships carried 400 passengers between Liverpool, New York, Belém, and Manaus. Almost as many to Iquitos. Now our ships have three two-berth cabins—and one of those is taken by the river pilots.

"I still love this run," the captain continued. "I've sailed lots of rivers—the Rajang in Borneo, the Pearl back of Hong Kong up to Canton. But the Amazon—now this is a *river.* You can't compare it to any other in the world. It's different every trip. And I'll bet it's the only run where going aground is not cause for dismissal. Been aground myself once. For 16 days. Occupational hazard, I call it."

This was a subject I wanted to ask about. From Leticia on we had navigation charts, but they had been published in 1958.

"I'm afraid you'll find them rather out-of-date," Captain Baxter said, as he led us into the chart room. There, an instrument was drawing squiggly lines on a moving roll of paper. "Recording fathometer," he explained. "Keep it operating most of the time when the river's going down, even in port." He indicated an area on a chart. "Here, for instance. A few years ago this was deep water. Now there's an island. Trees and grass all across the channel. Here's another place that used to be deep. Now there's a sand bar. We update our charts every run. Do you have a fathometer?"

"I'm the fathometer. I use a pole," Helen said with a mirthless smile.

"Well, you'd better use it a lot. And be ready to go astern when you touch bottom—going downriver the current can push you hard aground in seconds."

Feeling more sheepish by the moment, I explained that *Amazon Queen* didn't have reverse, that the rivermen we had spoken with in Pucallpa said we really didn't need it in a small boat.

"Well, old chap, all I can say is good luck. You've got a lot of river ahead of you. Your little boat is going to seem even smaller from here on."

Three hundred yards downstream from Leticia we entered Brazil, the only

Pancake-flat Surinam toad, Pipa pipa, *from Colombia rests on a floating leaf. Its unusual body, about 6 inches long, 4 inches wide, and 3/4-inch thick, helps disguise it from predators. Actually a frog, the Surinam lives almost entirely in the water. With no tongue to catch food, it grabs small animals from the mud with its forefeet.*

Portuguese-speaking country in South America. I had taken a crash course in the language before leaving Washington, but four months of speaking Spanish had obliterated almost everything I had learned. I took courage, however, from a statement José had made before we left Iquitos. "Don't worry, Señor Frank," he said, "Portuguese is only Spanish badly spoken."

At Benjamin Constant, Brazil's port of entry, I put this philosophy and what little I remembered of Portuguese to a test. The results were less than exhilarating. Fortunately the customs officer spoke Spanish too.

"Never mind," he encouraged. "You'll learn quickly. After all, Spanish is only Portuguese badly spoken."

"By the way," he added, "you'll need a flag for your *Amazon Queen.*" He presented us with a bright new ensign—blue globe in a yellow diamond against a green background with Brazil's motto, *Ordem e Progresso,* "Order and Progress," and a star to represent each state.

Shaggy three-toed sloths, Bradypus tridactylus *(opposite), idle in a Colombian grove; some sloths spend years in a single tree. An Indian girl upends a paca,* Agouti paca *(upper left); the rodent grows to about 30 inches long. A swamp deer,* Blastocerus dichotomus, *steps down a Belém park path. Below left, a bulky tapir,* Tapirus terrestris—*at about 600 pounds the biggest South American mammal—munches a mango. A piglike collared peccary,* Tayassu tajaçu, *investigates an exposed root.*

"Unlike any other river in the world—the Amazon is different every trip," says Capt. Philip Baxter, whose Booth Line ship M.V. Cyril (below right) berths to take on cargo at Leticia, the only Colombian port on the river. The leaky steamer Nariño (bottom), no longer fit for service on the Amazon, lies on a river terrace. The owners abandoned the craft in 1964. Today only a caretaker and his family live aboard.

In one important respect a great deal of progress has come to the Amazon since Lieutenant Herndon traveled down the river. In his time the Amazon was still closed to foreign vessels, and the American naval officer had to exchange his Peruvian-built craft for one of Brazilian construction. A circus company, floating downriver on a raft made of logs cut in Peru, was forced to build a new raft of Brazilian logs.

Such requirements ended in 1866 with the opening of the Amazon to vessels of all flags. However, we found that little else had changed. True, many of the villages that Herndon described as clusters of shacks have grown to towns of several thousand population, and electricity has come to some and to others paved streets.

But though a few affluent merchants zip around on motorbikes or in jeeps, most people still eke out a poor existence lumbering and collecting Brazil nuts, smoking wild rubber, fishing, and roasting cassava to make *farinha* — the coarse meal without which no Brazilian dinner is complete. The great development that Herndon so optimistically predicted would come once the Amazon was opened to foreign commerce has yet to be realized.

Indeed, if we accept Friar Carvajal's account, long stretches of the riverbanks were more heavily populated in 1542 than they are today: "... we saw the villages glimmering white, and we had not proceeded far when we saw coming up the river a great many canoes, all equipped for fighting, gaily colored, and [the men] with their shields on, which are made out of the shell-like skins of lizards and the hides of manatees and of tapirs, as tall as a man, because they cover them entirely."

By this time the Spaniards had built a second boat, larger than the first. Protected by the high gunwales of the two craft, with their thunder-spewing arquebuses and deadly accurate crossbows, Orellana's men drove off the Indians and captured a village where they found abundant food, "... enough to feed an expeditionary force of one thousand men for one year...."

If such a settlement actually existed, the second expedition to descend the river only 18 years later did not report it. The leader of the expedition, Lope de Aguirre, a mutineer and perhaps the most brutal cutthroat ever to sail the Amazon, wrote the King of Spain: "... the greater part of the shores being uninhabited.... I advise thee not to send any Spanish fleet up this ill-omened river ... if a hundred thousand men should go up, not one would escape, and there is nothing else to expect ... for the adventurers from Spain."

As we sailed past seemingly endless miles of jungle with their widely separated towns and villages and one-house farms, Helen and I found it difficult to credit either of the two accounts. The truth undoubtedly lies somewhere in between. If, in fact, Orellana did encounter large numbers of Indians, they may have fled deep into the jungle as the news of Lope de Aguirre's cruelty preceded him. Spanish and Portuguese colonists settling along the river in the 17th and 18th centuries sent the Indians retreating deeper and deeper into the forests. Herndon reported that the few Indians he saw were hardly distinguishable from the poorer-class mestizos. So it is today.

But what happened to those glimmering white cities? Perhaps, Helen and I reasoned, Carvajal was the victim of the same type of mirage that Herndon described: "... I thought I saw quite a large town, with houses of two or three

Wrestling a giant anaconda, Eunectes murinus, *Mike Tsalickis clasps the snake's head to prevent it from biting. Longest snakes in the world, anacondas sometimes grow to 38 feet and weigh up to 500 pounds. At right, a captive constrictor flicks its forked tongue to explore its surroundings. Contrary to popular belief, coiling anacondas kill not by crushing their victims, but by suffocating them. The nonpoisonous serpents seldom attack humans, preying mostly on fishes, mammals, and small amphibians.*

stories, built of stone and brick, with large heaps of white stone lying about in several places. There was a vessel lying off the town that I was satisfied was a large brig-of-war; but upon drawing near, my three-story houses dwindled to the smallest palm ranchos; my heaps of building stones to piles of egg-shells [the town's main occupation was rendering oil from turtle eggs]; and my man-of-war to a schooner of thirty tons."

So it was as Helen and I traveled down this great desert of a river flowing through an area no more densely populated than the Sahara. As with a desert mirage, islands on the far horizon seemed to hang suspended above the surface of the water, and reflections from the undulating brown water distorted our vision. We saw cities on high red banks where only a few stucco houses and a church stood. Cows grazing on the bank became as large as elephants.

But the daily growth of the Amazon was no mirage. Along the 1,000-mile stretch from Leticia to Manaus, hundreds of minor tributaries and dozens of larger ones—the Içá, Juruá, Japurá, Purus, major rivers in their own right—added their flow to the Amazon. The muddy waters spread wider and wider, and the rain squalls grew more frequent—the Amazon had assumed staggering proportions. As December faded into January, the rains came with increasing fury. We tried to ride out the first real storm and went hard aground when the wind ripples erased the guidelines of current. Tied to the *Queen* with long ropes, we jumped into the water and shoved off, pulling ourselves hand over hand back to the boat as it drifted into the channel. We needed only that one lesson; from then on we dashed for shore at the first sign of a squall.

Even in the shelter of a cove or the lee of a river bend, an Amazon storm is an awesome, overpowering spectacle of rampaging nature. Far away on the horizon, the sky purples. Thunder rumbles up the river, and the jungle whitens under shuddering sheets of lightning. The steady upriver breeze lulls and the jungle infuses the hot, still air with a rank, almost palpable odor of rotting leaves, logs, and damp earth. Blasts of wind, chilled by the sudden drop in barometric pressure, lower the temperature 20 degrees in seconds. Long rolling swells become roiling seas marbled with frothy whitecaps and flat sheets of spindrift. Raindrops beat a tattoo on *Amazon Queen*'s metal roof as the storm sweeps down upon us.

As fast as it comes, the storm passes. The sun bores through the overcast, spotlighting a patch of jungle with a green as soft and vibrant as a tourmaline seen through a jeweler's glass. Midst limply hanging leaves, still heavy under their hoard of platinum droplets, myriad insects resume their concert.

On our twenty-second day out of Leticia we reached the mouth of the Rio Negro, the Amazon's largest northern tributary. The inky black of the Negro and the silty mocha of the Amazon flowed side by side as far downriver as we could see. Raindrops bouncing off the river's surface changed from kernels of brown corn to silvery black pearls as we crossed the clearly defined confluence. Seven miles up the Negro, the city of Manaus shimmered through the great scrim of rain like a stage setting from the pageant of its own lost glory.

Nocturnal ocelot, Felis pardalis, *stalks the tropical forest. Outranked in size by two other Amazonian felines, the jaguar and the puma, the ocelot attains a head-and-body length of about 3 feet. Mottled chainlike markings run from head to tail.*

From Rubber Boom to Gold Rush: Bygone

CHAPTER EIGHT

THEY started arriving early at the opera house that late summer evening in 1910. Coaches clattered over broad avenues cobbled with stones imported from Portugal at a shilling apiece. Electric streetcars squealed along the 15 miles of track that webbed the city from the jungle's edge to the riverfront. A few Deutz automobiles—the agency had just opened—sputtered up the semicircular driveway to the redstone Teatro Amazonas. On the colonnaded portico ladies in Parisian gowns fanned themselves in the damp heat as their London-tailored escorts led them into the foyer. The heavy, dark furniture from England, carved in fanciful figures of jungle plants and vines, contrasted sharply with the Greek gods and goddesses frolicking on the frescoed ceilings.

In the Salão Nobre the select few attending the party preceding the opening-night performance of *Camille*—government officials, rubber barons, foreign dignitaries—drank celebratory toasts of champagne from Baccarat crystal and sampled caviar served on Limoges porcelain. Canvas murals between Venetian mirrors on the walls depicted jungle scenes, and if one stood at just the right angle, the Greek nymphs cavorting on the domed ceiling seemed to be watching the whole scene with amusement.

Ushers called, the houselights dimmed, and as the curtain rose, Domênico de Angelis's painted Venus seemed to float slowly upward from her Amazonian setting. A hushed murmur of excitement greeted the appearance of Lucília Peres, Brazil's foremost actress of the period. This was a night to remember, the gala opening of a celebrated play in an opera house any capital of Europe could claim with pride. It might have been London, Paris, or Rome; that it was jungle-girded Manaus, 1,200 miles up the Amazon, made it all the more remarkable. To the 50,000 people of the city, the two-million-dollar Teatro Amazonas symbolized a new prosperity that would never end.

Manaus had every reason to believe the good days were there to stay. The Amazon had a world monopoly on the ever-increasing rubber trade. The city fathers bypassed their competitors in Belém by encouraging ships to load raw rubber at the floating docks the British had built. Attracted by the boom, entrepreneurs from the United States, Europe, and South America had set up offices and built luxurious homes. Berlitz opened a language school, French

"Ostentatious, romantic, deceptive, and devoid of destiny," an observer once wrote of Manaus, a city whose fortunes after 1910 fell with the price of rubber. Made a free port in 1967 to stimulate development of the upper Amazon, the city now thrives again.

Elegance and Gun-Toting Prospectors

Homeward bound, a youngster climbs the steps leading up from a floating market in Manaus (opposite), carrying a load of limes and flopping fowl, including a domestic Muscovy duck. Above, a train of boats approaches the market. Strings of as many as 20 craft once plied the river, but now more families can afford their own outboard motors. These small trains assemble quickly and informally on the river, with boats latching on and dropping off every few miles. The authors sampled the wares of the bread vendor (left) and pronounced them "excellent, especially when still warm." Several floating markets line the waterfront of Manaus, but a large floating village, similar to crowded Belén at Iquitos, has been declared unsanitary and disbanded.

modistes and British tailors did brisk business, and in sidewalk cafes string quartets played Liszt. The city claimed to be the richest per capita in the Americas. The men who gathered daily between three and four in the afternoon to check world rubber quotations knew little and cared less how much suffering went into every diamond they bought and every glass of wine they drank. They knew only that rubber could pay to send their laundry to London for washing and their children to Paris for schooling.

If the boom was sudden, the bust was even more so, though its seeds had been sprouting—literally—for a long time. In 1876, twenty years before Manaus opened its opera house, an Englishman in Santarém, about halfway between Manaus and Belém, quietly had gathered 70,000 of the best *Hevea* seeds he could find. Henry Alexander Wickham is still considered a scoundrel and a smuggler by many Brazilians, but he did nothing wrong; no law prohibited the export of rubber seeds. The seedlings, nurtured in London's Kew Gardens and transplanted to Asia by the grove, soon guaranteed the collapse of the Amazonian rubber industry, focused as it was on the inefficient and comparatively costly tapping of trees in the wild.

In 1910, the peak year for Manaus, 38,000 tons of rubber were shipped from the Amazon, compared with only 8,000 from Asian plantations. Two years later Asia's share of the world market had jumped to 28,000 tons, and by 1915 it had nearly quadrupled. The price of rubber fell accordingly, leaving the city in panic. The opera house closed its doors, the fine houses were boarded up, and the cabaret girls, modistes, tailors, and foreign rubber merchants departed almost as quickly as they had come. Manaus—and every other town along the Amazon—drifted back into its pre-boom lethargy.

Helen and I found Manaus somewhere between boom and bust all over again. Established as a duty- and tax-free zone in 1967, the city had seen its population grow to 300,000. Screeching brakes and blasting horns rasped through the streets with traffic-jam intensity. Foreign businessmen were back in volume as representatives for European, American, and Japanese manufacturers. Some 2,000 new shops had opened to sell imported goods ranging from outboard motors to cameras, fans, television sets, and air conditioners. Brazilian tourists flocked to Manaus to pick up bargain items, in many cases with the intention of reselling them at a profit in the southern part of the country.

A thriving trade in contraband developed. To control it the government suddenly removed electrical appliances—the items most in demand—from the $100 duty-free allowance Brazilians could take out of the city. The flow of tourists dwindled. Deprived of their principal customers, with the Manaus market already saturated and with millions of dollars worth of merchandise on hand, many of the new businesses were closing. Then, just as suddenly, the government removed the crippling restriction to give merchants a chance to unload their stocks.

"It's this sort of indecision that holds Manaus back," one businessman complained. "Who's going to invest money here when no one knows what the government will do from day to day? Everyone is just waiting."

Not everyone. Issac Sabbá, Amazonia's leading industrialist, was busily adding gold and iron mining, a shipyard, and a river transportation company to his complex that already included processing plants for rosewood oil,

Mosaic waves lap at the marble-colonnaded entrance of the Teatro Amazonas in Manaus, completed in 1896 to satisfy the booming city's thirst for culture. European opera companies, imported at great expense, risked malaria and dysentery to sing here. The plaza statue commemorates the opening of the Brazilian Amazon to ships of all nations.

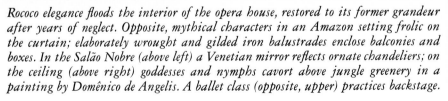

Rococo elegance floods the interior of the opera house, restored to its former grandeur after years of neglect. Opposite, mythical characters in an Amazon setting frolic on the curtain; elaborately wrought and gilded iron balustrades enclose balconies and boxes. In the Salão Nobre (above left) a Venetian mirror reflects ornate chandeliers; on the ceiling (above right) goddesses and nymphs cavort above jungle greenery in a painting by Domênico de Angelis. A ballet class (opposite, upper) practices backstage.

On the feast day of St. Sebastian — celebrated on January 20 — a crowd congregates (below) for the rites of macumba, *a cult similar to the* obeah *of the West Indies. Originally brought to Brazil by slaves from central Africa, the eclectic macumba rituals reflect a mixture of pagan and Christian beliefs. Dancing to throbbing drums, participants in the sacred ceremonies — like the woman at left — experience an emotional release. Mediums achieve a trancelike state and convey to devotees the wisdom of the gods — answering personal questions on jobs, lovers, or financial affairs.*

rubber, jute, and Brazil nuts, an oil refinery, and a supermarket. Starting with nothing in 1921, Senhor Sabbá has built a business empire that grosses, by his own estimate, some 40 million dollars a year. In his spacious, modern home near the old opera house, he presented the free zone in a different, more optimistic light:

"The zone was not set up to attract adventurers who want to make a quick fortune and leave," he said. "It was set up to lower the cost of living here and to provide employment. But most important, it was set up to attract industry. The government has created the perfect plan for development. Now it is up to the individual. Businessmen in the south of Brazil can invest half their taxes in approved Amazon projects instead of paying that money to the government. They pay no income taxes on their earnings until 1982 and no federal consumer taxes until 1997. The opportunity and incentives are here."

With such incentives industry is starting to move into Manaus. A 60,000-ton steel mill is nearing completion, and a jewelry factory is already in production. Some 30 other projects have been approved for the city by SUDAM —Superintendency for the Development of the Amazon—the new agency set up to administer the development program. There is even a luxury hotel on the drawing boards, complete with a huge plastic bubble to air-condition a portion of the adjacent jungle.

As we prepared to resume our journey aboard *Amazon Queen,* I thought back to what Lieutenant Herndon had written 117 years earlier under similar circumstances. "Having had my boat thoroughly repaired, calked, and well fitted with palm coverings..." Herndon had related, "with a sort of Wandering-Jew feeling that I was destined to leave every body behind and never to stop, I sailed from Barra [Manaus] on the eighteenth of February."

On another February day, as Helen and I sat on the promenade deck of the Booth Line freighter *Viajero* sipping rum punches and saying goodbye to the friends we had met in Manaus, Herndon's lament struck a sympathetic chord. The ship's officers in gold braid and crisp whites, the Booth Line officials in casual sport clothes, their wives in chic linen dresses only reinforced the feeling that we too were about to leave civilization behind. We kept looking toward the confluence of the Rio Negro and the Amazon that spread before us. In seven months we had traveled 3,000 miles; only the 1,100 miles to Belém remained. Yet the river seemed even more interminable than ever.

I had spent the last week refitting *Amazon Queen,* having her hull checked for leaks and repainted, installing a bilge pump, and replacing the propeller shaft's makeshift wooden bearings with proper marine bearings. More important, we had added a simple neutral gear that allowed us to start the engine before casting off into the current—an addition that would prove crucial when tidal forces added their strength to the Amazon. The *Queen* had taken a few more steps toward becoming a ship equal to her name, but she still seemed like a minnow beside a whale as we pulled away from the *Viajero.* The captain honored her with three blasts on the whistle, the traditional *bon voyage* from one ship to another, and we sailed for Santarém.

Reluctant to face the Amazon's mosquitoes any sooner than necessary, we beached the *Queen* early that night in a lovely white sand cove on the insect-free Rio Negro side of the confluence. As though *(Continued on page 170)*

"Little Ben"—a gift of the British Government—tolls the hours on Avenida Eduardo Ribeiro in Manaus (opposite). Establishing Manaus as a free port in 1967 brought immediate expansion: By midsummer of 1968 every month saw dozens of new businesses opening their doors, and the city's population approached 300,000. At right, youngsters at a bus stop hawk packets of fried banana chips —prepared at home by their mothers—to early-morning commuters. Below, three boys cavort in a fountain fronting the cathedral.

167

"Wedding of the waters" unites the Rio Negro, left, with the mud-brown Amazon. The two flow side

by side for about 50 miles before the Amazon finally prevails over its largest black-water tributary.

separated by an invisible membrane, the black-water Rio Negro and brown Amazon flowed side by side. Some 50 miles downstream the Amazon would triumph over the Negro, but not by diluting it. The black water would just sink from sight. Scientists have not affirmed why the two do not mix, although differences in water density may be one answer. Unlike the muddy Amazon, the Rio Negro—whose water appears black but turns to the color of weak tea when scooped up in a glass—flows through sandy soil, picking up almost no silt.

Even more remarkable, the shores of the Negro remain almost free of insects. Biologist Carroll M. Williams of Harvard University, a leader of the 1967 Scripps Institution of Oceanography Amazon expedition, theorizes that during high water the slow-moving Rio Negro spreads out into the bordering jungles, dissolving vegetable matter and carrying off plant juices and sap. The dissolved matter seems to inhibit insect growth and reproduction, making the Rio Negro, in effect, an inexhaustible supply of natural insecticide. Whether further investigation will substantiate Dr. Williams' theory or not, Helen and I had found all along the river that moorings near black-water tributaries and lakes were invariably freer of mosquitoes than the Amazon itself.

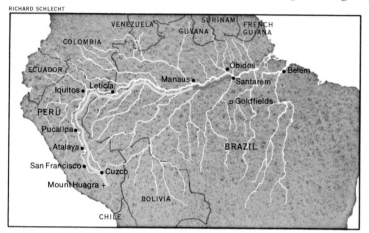

RICHARD SCHLECHT

Glitter of gold—in monuments of another era's wealth in Manaus, in the fields near Santarém—beckons the authors.

During much of the seven-day voyage dark skies and rain threatened to develop into the fierce February storms that so often forced Herndon to run for shelter. Increased by the heavy flows of the Negro and Madeira rivers, the Amazon below Manaus widens in places to seven miles. Sometimes it took an hour just to cross the river as we followed the channel from one side to the other, and when the full force of the gusty winds caught us in the middle, we rocked and pitched as though we were at sea. Each time the channel-marking current lines disappeared in a mass of foaming whitecaps we blessed Rogelio Marinho, the veteran river pilot in Manaus who had spent hours with us, updating our charts and locating the new shoals that had formed.

Rogelio also had plotted a small-boat course through narrow, sheltered channels. Whenever possible we left the turbulent mainstream and cruised those canal-like glassy waters—waters so deep that Helen was able to abandon her perch on the bow and relax beside me at the helm for the first time since leaving Iquitos.

More populated than any area we had yet seen on the river, the steep, high banks shimmered through the rain and mist with the fresh green of jute. Mile after mile of the reedlike, tufted stalks waved in regular ranks along the banks, a small part of the fledgling boom that has made the lower Amazon the fourth-largest producer of jute in the world.

Jute, like pepper, was introduced by Japanese immigrants, but the *caboclos,* or local farmers, are enthusiastically cultivating it too. Under leaden skies, their houses on stilts, their small pastures for cattle, their groves of papaya, cassava, and bananas, made a long, low mosaic of greens and yellows against a backdrop of towering jungle.

Many of the new jute growers had been subsistence farmers who had never known a cash crop except for what Brazil nuts and rubber they could gather. Those we spoke to radiated an optimism we rarely experienced in our travels down the Amazon.

"This is only temporary," one farmer said, showing us his cane-and-thatch dwelling. "Soon I'll build a new house of wood, with a metal roof."

I hoped he was right. The jute industry, which supplies the materials to make bags for Brazil's coffee, is already suffering competition from plastic bags manufactured in the south of the country. If the trend continues, jute may go the way of rubber in providing hope for the Amazon's future.

Reaching Santarém — 480 miles below Manaus — we found the attractive, Portuguese-colonial town at the mouth of the Tapajós River caught up in a minor boom of its own. An epidemic of gold fever had hit the area.

"It's really wild, like reliving history, like the rush of '49 in California," Sam Rimpel, a young American prospector told us. "Until a few months ago, when the government started controls, the *garimpeiros* — the prospectors — were selling gold right here in the streets. The man who made the first strike came out of the *garimpos,* the goldfields, with three five-gallon oilcans full of nuggets and dust. Half a million dollars' worth. Spent it all in a year. But there's lots more still up there."

"Up there" is a two-hour flight by light plane south from Santarém. Leaving Helen, Balty, and the *Queen* sandwiched between a barge loaded with moaning cattle and a boatful of itinerant rock musicians practicing for a dance that night, I took off with Sam and Luiz Mendonça, a Brazilian pilot who had been ferrying garimpeiros and their supplies between Santarém and the goldfields for six years. As the single-engine Cessna taxied onto the runway, Luiz crossed himself and tightened his seat belt. I reached for my seat belt too. No seat belt.

"Don't worry," Sam laughed, "Luiz is one of the best pilots in the garimpos. He's logged more than 5,000 hours over these jungles."

Luiz's battered plane looked as if it had logged at least that many hours since its last overhaul. But it was too late to worry. Already we were circling Santarém — the pastel profile of the town rising behind the congested harbor. Below us dhowlike boats from Belém scudded across the clear water under red or blue sails. Canoes rocked in the white wake of smoke-spewing diesel riverboats. Bullock-drawn carts plodded along the bank toward the morning market, and omnipresent black buzzards drifted down from their night-time roosts on the red tile roofs.

For an hour we paralleled the Tapajós, surely one of the most beautiful rivers in the Amazon Basin with its white-sand beaches, deep coves, and clear water. We flew over Belterra, then Fordlandia, both part of Henry Ford's attempt to produce his own rubber by developing Asian-style plantations. Starting in 1927, Ford built model towns, hospitals, power plants, recreation facilities, sawmills, and roads. He cleared nearly 50,000 acres of jungle and planted some 3½ million trees imported from the Philippines. In 19 years he spent 15 million dollars, but achieved little success. When planted close together

Exercising gymnasts (opposite) pattern the courtyard of the Instituto de Educação do Amazonas, a school in Manaus; spikes on the wall discourage intruders. Almost 6,000 students attend the institute, a structure that stretches an entire city block. At left, Aria Ramos cradles her silent violin. Daughter of an important Manaus family, Aria died at carnival time in 1915 when a reveler, dressed as an American cowboy, fired his "unloaded" pistol; townspeople donated money for this tomb. Below left, a bikinied bather steps toward Ponta Negra beach, a 15-minute taxi ride upriver from Manaus. At a nearby waterfall (below) swimmers cling to a rocky ledge.

Doorway on the Amazon frames a mother and her children, pensively watching the world drift slowly past their riverfront home. During high water their house on stilts (third from right, below) barely escapes inundation. Men of the settlement — mainly laborers and fishermen who work out of Manaus — commute daily by canoe.

Brazilian rubber trees quickly succumb to a debilitating leaf disease found only in the Amazon. After a brief spurt of activity during World War II when the Japanese cut off Asian sources of rubber, Ford gave up. He sold everything to the Brazilian Government for $250,000.

At a few experimental stations near Manaus, and at Goodyear's well maintained plantation near Belém, rubber specialists are continuing the search for disease-resistant strains. In the meantime Brazil imports rubber from Asia, and Belterra and Fordlandia wither away, producing at less than a tenth of their capacities. We dropped down over great gaps in the rectangular pattern of groves where sick rubber trees had been cleared to make pasture for cattle. Machinery lay rusting by shabby shops. The model towns seemed overgrown, the straight grid of their streets returning again to the jungle.

From Fordlandia we headed south, away from the Tapajós toward the Xingu River, across low, jungled hills reputed to be the territory of some of Brazil's most savage Indians.

"Not any more," Sam said. "The garimpeiros ran them all out. They're more savage than the Indians. Hardly a week passes that there isn't a killing."

Another hour at 140 knots brought us to São Domingos' garimpo, a cream-colored, sandy opening in the jungle near a shantytown of grass huts. A mile or so away a narrow strip about 200 yards long had been cleared on the top of a low ridge. At first I thought it was another goldfield, but Luiz assured me that it

Armed against claim-jumpers and bandits, a prospector sluices for gold south of Santarém. A free-for-all rush has lured scores of men to the site of the strike. Living in a squalid shantytown and in constant fear of robbers, they earn about $75 a month, almost triple the average wage paid laborers in Santarém. At right, successful garimpeiros display their reward: a pinch of gleaming metal in their sluice pan. A patrón measures 100 grams of gold onto his scales (below). Patrones stake claims to large tracts, hire prospectors to work them, and collect a hefty percentage of the take.

was the runway. He pointed out two wrecked planes as proof of his statement.

"Couldn't repair those," he said. "Four others cracked up here too. But after some first aid they made it back to Santarém. We call this strip the garimpo-pilot proving ground."

With that comforting remark Luiz crossed himself again, cinched up his seat belt, and shoved the controls forward. The plane nosed steeply down toward the low end of the airstrip for an uphill landing. My body rose in the seat, my stomach seemingly leading the way, and when the wheels touched the rough earth the plane hopped higher yet.

By the time we rolled to a stop just short of the trees I was convinced: Anyone who could land on that runway *had* to be good. I hoped the takeoff would be equally convincing.

São Domingos is one of the older garimpos. Claims near the airstrip had been worked out long ago, and we walked a half hour through hilly forest to reach the nearest digs. The trail was littered with spent .38-caliber shells, and almost everyone we met wore a revolver strapped to his waist.

"Where's yours?" I asked Sam jokingly.

"Back in the plane," Sam replied, "and I feel kind of naked right now. When I'm at my own claim I wear a .357 Magnum every minute. It's beside me in my hammock when I sleep too."

The shantytown we had seen from the air became even more grim at close range. Most of the shacks were given over to bars offering beer at $1.75 a bottle. Eggs were 50 cents apiece, rice 75 cents a pound. Girls and women lounged in little cubicles of thatch and cane. A goldsmith fashioned watchbands and rings from pea-size nuggets.

Beyond the village the trail opened onto a horrible sore in the earth. Scattered over a jungle-ringed clearing several acres in area were a series of 30-foot-square pits awash with water channeled from a nearby stream. Piles of gray overburden bulged from the torn ground like so many boils.

About 20 men worked the claim, some shoveling the gold-bearing sand into long sluice boxes, others pouring water into *cobras fumandos,* or smoking snakes —crude sieves that neither smoked nor looked like snakes. In every pit at least one man wore a gun. Each looked up when we approached, saw we were not armed, and went back to work. I wondered how much these men earned to suffer the living conditions I had seen back in the village, to spend their days grubbing ankle-deep in mud and their nights in fear that someone would steal what they had dug.

"About $75 a month," Sam said, "almost three times what they can make back in Santarém. Very few are independents. Most work for some richer garimpeiro or the patrón who claims the land. They get a wage and a percentage of the gold. But prospectors are all alike. Everybody expects to strike it rich."

"What about you, Sam?" I asked. "Is this the way you do it?"

"Not me. I'm working the rivers with portable suction pumps and diving gear. These waters have never been touched commercially. I'm moving my equipment to another claim now. Not set up yet. But when I am, I'll find gold. I'm not worried about that. I'm more worried about what'll happen when I do find it. Where can I get a bodyguard I can trust to get the gold from my claim to the airstrip?"

Sudden downpour catches a canoe in midstream at sunrise. "In seven months we had traveled 3,000 miles on the Amazon; only the 1,100 miles to Belém remained," the Schreiders wrote, as the river broadened dramatically at the confluence with the Rio Negro just below Manaus. "Yet the river seemed even more interminable than ever."

Journey's End: A Harrowing Episode on

URING MY VISIT to the goldfields, Helen had been doing a little prospecting of her own—for iron. Noting that the boats around her were equipped with anchors, she set out to learn why. Below Santarém, the rivermen told her, the Amazon—*Rio Mar,* River Sea, they called it—rises and falls with the tide. Unless we could find deepwater moorings at villages along the way, we would have to anchor some distance from the bank. The old-fashioned, hand-forged anchor we found in a Santarém boatyard looked big enough for the *Queen Elizabeth,* but we bought it anyway and hoped we wouldn't need it.

Our hopes proved overly optimistic. The thunderheads and thrashing winds that had been building for weeks caught us two days below Santarém. Swollen by the Tapajós and Trombetas and a score of smaller streams, the Amazon had indeed become a river sea. We headed for the closest land, dipping and rolling in the troughs. Reaching a protected cove, we were preparing to tie up in a large clump of reeds when a caboclo ran from his hut to warn us that the tide was going out. If we remained we soon would be aground, he called.

It did not seem possible that the tidal effect could be so strong 500 miles upriver from the sea, but we had learned long ago to trust the advice of the local people. Under a black sky thick with rain we shoved off into the deep, turbulent water. Some 25 yards from the bank I heaved the anchor overboard, paid out 30 feet of chain, and felt the flukes catch as the current swung us downstream. The river fell swiftly. What we had thought were reeds turned out at low tide to be the tops of small trees 8 to 10 feet high. Our sheltering cove had become a patch of black mud.

The storm raged all night, keeping us awake checking our anchorage. Even so we were startled when the bow began to slant sharply downward. Rain slashed into the cabin, and the wind snatched the door from my hand as I climbed out to investigate. The river was rising again, taking up the slack in the anchor chain and threatening to pull the bow under. Water was near the gunwales by the time I slacked off enough to let the *Queen* bob freely. Come morning we found that we had swung a full 360 degrees with the wind, current, and tide. But the anchor had held.

Each of the next nine days to Belém the Rio Mar taught us something new.

Amazonian version of a gunter-rigged fishing sloop follows an inshore channel, nearly brushing a wall of dense jungle. Below Óbidos, where the river broadens and tides from the Atlantic first become noticeable, sailboats, or alvarengas, *appear by the hundred.*

the Storm-Tossed Amazon

Brahmans bolt across swampy pastureland on Marajó Island in the Amazon's 200-mile-wide estuary.

Largely devoted to grazing, the eastern half of the island supports some 400,000 head of cattle.

As we drew closer to the sea, the tides grew stronger, and our progress varied from hour to hour. When the incoming tide countered the current, we barely made headway. When the tide was running, we sped along at 12 to 14 knots. Sometimes the upriver wind gusted against the current, kicking up waves higher than *Amazon Queen,* forcing us to throttle back or plunge along while a steady brown deluge hammered over the bow and rattled the steamy pilot-house windows. Gradually we began to feel an exhilaration in the way the sturdy little *Queen* handled the waves.

Approaching the mouth of the Amazon, we reached the point where the river splits around Marajó Island, a mass of swampy land almost as large as Switzerland. Here Orellana had taken the northern channel, made it to Trinidad, then to Spain, and eventually returned to the shores of the New World as governor of Amazonas. For 11 months he searched in vain for the main channel of the Amazon, and then he died, no one knows just where. José Toribio Medina, Orellana's most generous chronicler, closes the story:

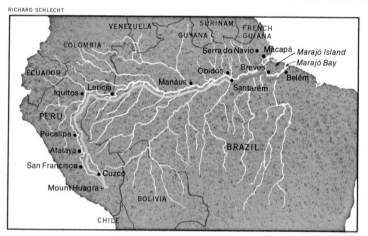

Amazon Queen nears the Atlantic, then becomes caught in a storm on the way to Belém, the largest city on the river.

"Buried at the foot of one of those aged trees of the always verdant forests bathed by the current of the majestic river which he had discovered, he at last found rest from his toils and sufferings in the midst of that luxuriant nature which was a sepulcher worthy of his imperishable name."

Lieutenant Herndon took the southern channel. He reached Belém, returned to the United States, and was given command of the mail ship *Central American,* plying between New York and Panama. He later went down with his vessel in a storm off Cape Hatteras, North Carolina.

We chose to follow Herndon's route, turning into the "Narrows," a series of tight, twisting channels between Marajó Island and the southern bank of the Amazon. After five days of unremitting rolling and pitching, we welcomed the calm waters. But at the same time the grim jungle to either side depressed us. Though much of the Amazon's export lumber is cut here, the forest seems untouched, with trees and vines struggling for footing in the flooded earth.

When spring tides rush in, the river level may rise 15 to 18 feet in two or three hours. As the river rises so do the people. Terrestrial at low water, they become amphibious at half tide, sloshing about calf-deep in mud. And when the river is highest, they turn arboreal, perching among the trees atop their houses on stilts.

Most of the inhabitants chip out a meager existence cutting logs for sawmills and plywood factories downriver, supplementing their poor diet of fish and beans with a few vegetables grown in earth-filled wooden trays kept out of reach of floodwaters. Nothing seems permanent, nothing substantial, as though everyone is waiting, always waiting, for the next tide to wash him away.

The people accepted us as they accepted life—without emotion. Each night when we approached the crude piers built out over the water, they helped us tie up. They warned us of submerged logs, showed us the deep water, and taught us to loop our bow and stern lines around their mooring posts—loose enough to slide up and down with the tide, snug enough to hold us when the swift current reversed its flow. With reserved pride they accepted the canned food we offered and returned to their huts and their waiting.

On one occasion they had waited too long. Lost in a labyrinth of channels, we stopped a canoe for directions. A wan and frail little girl of 5 or 6 lay limply under the palm canopy. Her parents had paddled all day to Breves to find a doctor, but the doctor had been away. We wondered if he could have saved the child even had he been there. Her fleshless limbs, pinched face, splotchy, translucent skin, and distended stomach signaled advanced malnutrition. I asked how long the child had been ill. Two weeks, a month, the father wasn't sure. We gave them canned milk and vitamins, but the child was too weak to swallow. Helpless, frustrated, we watched them paddle away. A few days, a week earlier … but what are days or weeks or even months on the Amazon? Time is when the river rises or when the sun sets or when the rains come. Time is when a child dies.

At 0943 hours, March 5, 1969, *Amazon Queen* sailed from the Narrows into the Bay of Mouths, 152 miles from Belém. It was one of those rare, breathless mornings with high, light clouds reflected mirror-perfect in the sun-tinted water. The scores of low islands to our right appeared like ink smudges on a piece of paper and the horizon an obscure crease between sea and sky. Under limp, blue sails a trading boat drifted with the current. *Rio Camenta,* one of the last wood-burning passenger steamers on the Amazon, left us in a pall of black smoke, her decks a net of bright hammocks so closely hung that they had to swing in harmony. We followed a tanker through the intricate channel north of the Shoals of Otelo where six ships had sunk. Suggestive of grave markers on a flat, brown prairie, the masts and funnels of two of the vessels still poked above the surface of the water. With growing excitement we checked off each landmark on the chart, recording when the tides and current changed and how they affected our progress.

Except for a few brief rain squalls, March 7 also began perfectly, but once the tide changed we found that *Amazon Queen* could not buck the incoming current. Though it was only midday, we turned into the Rio Atuá, a small stream flowing south out of Marajó Island, the last rock-free anchorage before Belém. We moored at a sawmill and spent the rest of the afternoon checking the motor, gasoline filter, and bilge pump for the final run across Marajó Bay.

The tide was almost full when we awakened at 0430. Her deck level with the pier, the *Queen* tugged at her mooring lines. Bits of debris were still floating upstream, and the air had just a touch of the sea to it. In the dead calm, steam rose in a thin wisp from my coffee as I waited for Balty to climb aboard after his morning excursion.

In the cabin Helen was plotting a compass course to Belém, 66 miles away. It seemed odd—a compass course for a river—but where we would cross the bay, the river stretched nearly 17 miles from bank to bank. At the moment I was more concerned about the channel leading into the bay. Rocks on both

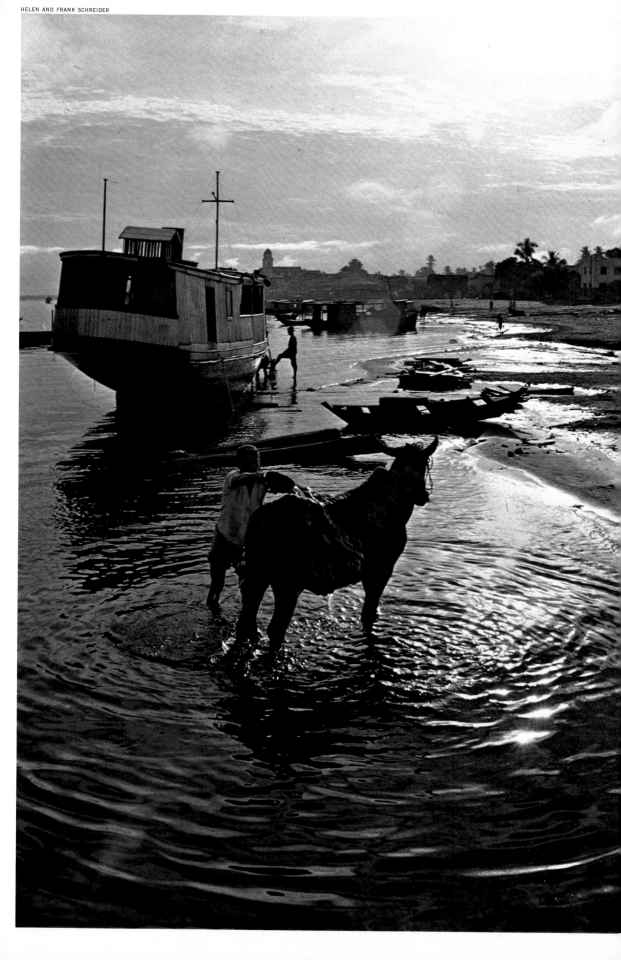

Early-rising Santarém cargo-cart owner bathes his ox in the tranquil Tapajós River; they will spend the day supplying wharfside boats in the Portuguese-colonial city. At a riverfront market (below), vendors chat while black vultures scavenge for scraps of fish or other edible refuse. At bottom, ocean-going steamers berth in Santarém's harbor, 700 miles up the Amazon from the Atlantic, to take on cargo and passengers.

sides narrowed the five-mile-wide river to a two-mile corridor with little room to maneuver should a storm come up. And once under way we could not turn back against the current. But the moon was between full and dark—the calmest time of the month, rivermen had often assured me. I sniffed the air; there was none of the electric tension that customarily precedes an Amazon storm.

The sky was beginning to brighten in the east. The mooring lines were slack, the current about to turn. The motor started smoothly with the first pull on the rope. We cast off in semidarkness and steered at idling speed through the narrow mouth of Atuá into the main river. It was 0610, March 8, our last day aboard *Amazon Queen.*

Helen handed me the course she had plotted—20 minutes at 140°, 90 minutes at 090°, 50 minutes at 073°, 22 minutes at 063°, 70 minutes at 046°. The last course should bring us in sight of the beacon on the far side of Marajó Bay; from there we would be able to navigate by sight.

Soon after we turned to 090°, the first flush of dawn diffused into a heavy overcast, reducing our visibility. But Helen had done a good job; we passed the first beacon on schedule and right on course. A light breeze had sprung up, raising long swells. With her spare fuel drums almost empty, *Amazon Queen* rolled lightly, responding quickly to our course changes. She was a good little ship, and we would be sorry to part with her. But we knew that Father Louis, an American priest we had met in Santarém, would take good care of her. Towed back upriver, she would be of help to him with his work on the tranquil Tapajós. At 0912 we sighted Manteiga Beacon through a light rain. The current had carried us too close to the rocks, and we changed course, heading for the center of the channel again, cutting through white-peaked waves under heavy, purple skies. We closed the pilothouse windows and turned into the 046° leg of our course. At 0930 we made the last entry in our log: "Well into open water of Marajó Bay. Closest land estimated 8 miles away but visible only from crest of waves. Wind strong. Rain heavy. Visibility dropping to 300 yards. Water breaking over bow continuously. Some flooding around pilothouse windows. Helen manning bilge pump."

Bucking and plunging, *Amazon Queen* burrowed through the waves, riding the crests one moment, dropping 8 to 10 feet into the troughs the next. Throttling back, swinging the wheel, I yawed the *Queen,* taking the waves at an angle to minimize their force. The short, high chop tossed the stern clear of the water on each crest. The propeller raced in the air, and the rudder provided no control. Using the "roller coaster" technique we had learned in our amphibious-jeep days, I throttled back still more when the *Queen* tilted down into the troughs, increased the speed as she climbed to the crests, and throttled back to coast her over the top. Again I began to sense that exhilaration as the *Queen* responded, tucking down her stern on command, spurting ahead, slowing, spurting ahead once more.

Gauging each wave through the fogged windows, I kept the *Queen* zigzagging along her course. Water still flooded in with each wave, but as long as Helen kept pumping I knew the *Queen* could take anything the Amazon could dish out. Then Helen called: Water was rising in the bilge; the pump had stopped working.

Helen took the wheel while I checked. Even back in the engine room I heard the waves smashing over the bow. Spurting through *(Continued on page 194)*

Treacherous waves thrash the pilothouse of Amazon Queen *as a storm churns Mara-jó Bay, 17 miles wide at this point. At the height of the blow the boat's bilge pump clogged; water flooded the engine, and the powerless craft nearly sank. After a terrifying hour and 15 minutes, the Schreiders maneuvered to the safety of Belém's harbor.*

HELEN AND FRANK SCHREIDER

Cottonball cumuli drift above the Amazon's last labyrinth, the mighty river's immense estuary; channels and tributaries flow from Caviana Island, feeding the broad but shallow Canal Perigoso — Dangerous Canal. The famed pororoca, *or "big roar" (opposite), rushes inland from the Atlantic Ocean. Such tidal bores — born of clashes between flood tides and the opposing river current — sweep in at 10 to 15 miles per hour.*

Gaily colored masts of fishing boats spin delicate webs of rigging in the busy port of Belém. In a waterfront medicine stall crowded with jungle remedies (below), a dark-haired vendor proffers a dried snakeskin; the buyer may cut it into strips for wrapping charms made of herbs, bones, and feathers. Cigarette pack-size boxes (lower left) contain defumações—*scents extracted from aromatic roots, oils, barks, and blossoms. A youth (lower right) counters a park lion's glower with a broad smile.*

cracks around the windows where the uncured wood had shrunk, the water rushed aft under the floorboards to the sump. I felt my stomach knot up. I was afraid, sick afraid, more afraid than Helen, perhaps, because I knew what all that water swirling in the boat could do. The water was an inch or so below the engine flywheel. I tried the pump. It swished, sucking air.

I told Helen to head for the nearest land ... But the rocks ... Never mind the rocks ... We're taking on too much water ... If we hit a wave wrong ... If all this water rushes over the engine....

I reached into the sump, felt for the bilge-pump strainer and pulled out a wad of hair. Balty's hair — the sump was full of it. When I had checked the day before, it had been clean. And the *Queen* was swept every day too. But in all

HELEN AND FRANK SCHREIDER (UPPER) AND NATIONAL GEOGRAPHIC PHOTOGRAPHER WINFIELD PARKS

Beauty and the beast on the lower Amazon: A bikini-clad water-skier slaloms grace-fully during a Sunday outing from the Yacht Club in Belém, the thriving social and cultural center of northern Brazil. A lassoed caiman, caught skulking for cattle, struggles in rage and terror in a water hole on Marajó Island. The sophisticated and the primitive, existing side by side, lend mystery to the area; two hours upriver from the skyscrapers and freeways of Belém, a lush wilderness waits unchanged.

those months of shedding, each day a few hairs had sifted through the cracks between the floorboards where we couldn't see them, clumping between the ribs. Now they had been flushed back to the sump with the *Queen's* rearing and bucking. I remembered a day off the coast of Panama in an amphibious jeep years before when another shedding German shepherd had clogged a bilge pump. But that day had been calm and sunny with land in sight, and we had joked about foolish people who took dogs along on boats.

I unscrewed the strainer valve, started to clean it, then dropped it as the rearing *Queen* threw me off balance. Another rush of water filled the sump, flooding around the air-cooling fan of the engine. Steam sizzled from the exhaust pipe. Boiling water spattered from the cylinder and spark plug. The motor sputtered, coughed, sputtered again, and died.

Without power, without control, the *Queen* swung broadside, rolling in the trough. The water, now almost a foot deep in the bilge, surged from side to side with the waves, heeling us over more each time. The fuel drums on the stern deck were sliding, adding their weight to the rolling. When the wind and waves outside and the water inside hit resonance, when they all worked together...we were already heeling over to the port or starboard windows with each roll...a strong gust, a high wave at the wrong time....

Strangely calm, Helen left the wheel and started bailing. I fished in the sump for the strainer valve. The *Queen* was rolling too much to stand. We sat hunched in the little engine room. In the cabin pots and dishes clattered to the deck. Books fell from the shelves. The stove grated across the table. The wind drove through the shutters, and waves thumped against the side, breaking over the cabin roof. But less water came in as we wallowed in the trough. Bailing as fast as she could, Helen kept pace. The level stayed constant, even fell a little. I refitted the cleaned strainer valve and primed the pump. Pumping and bailing we cleared the bilge. I sprayed the spark plug, breaker points, and wiring with the fire extinguisher to displace the water, waited a few minutes for the carbon tetrachloride to evaporate, and wound the rope around the starter pulley. I yanked. The pop-pop that throbbed through the *Amazon Queen* no longer sounded like a profanity. It was a benediction.

Stepping over broken glass, cutlery, saturated books and charts, cameras and lenses tossed from their case when it fell, I took the wheel while Helen cleared the shambles. It was 1045. The storm had lasted an hour and 15 minutes — the longest hour and 15 minutes I can ever remember.

At 1300 we sighted the beacon marking the channel to Belém, and a little while later the white skyscrapers of the largest city on the Amazon hove into view. At 1500 we dropped anchor at the Belém Yacht Club. With speedboats and water-skiers buzzing like hornets across the calm, sheltered water, I squeezed Helen's hand. "Well, this is it. We made it."

"No, we didn't make it," she replied softly. "The river just let us go."

The Amazon had let us go. But what had it taught us? That it is the greatest river in the world? There was never any question. That it is the longest river as well? Perhaps.

But the Amazon had taught us far far more. Still, as I stood at the window of our 17-story hotel, I felt a flood of contradictions welling up within me and my thoughts became as entwined and confused as the jungles we had lived in for

Erupting in a frenzy of fun and a riot of color, Belém merrymakers jam a ballroom during Carnaval, *the annual pre-Lenten celebration observed throughout Brazil. Below, a costumed street dancer competes for prizes and prestige as drummers in high hats pount out a pulsating, hypnotic beat. Beginning officially on the Sunday before Ash Wednesday, the festivities run for three days, curtailing business activities.*

8½ months. Was this part of the Amazon—this cosmopolitan city of 625,000 where we dined on lobster thermidor, drank fine wine, and slept in air-conditioned bliss, and awakened each morning to see children roller-skating and maids pushing perambulators around the bronze statue of liberty in the plaza below us? The six lanes of traffic that raced past white obelisks of apartments and offices rising to 26 stories—was this part of the Amazon too? Farther away, the robotlike silhouettes of dock cranes leaned over ships in the harbor, ships that would sail for Europe, the United States, Asia, and other parts of South America. On the other side of town 1,400 miles of new highway throbbed with truck traffic between Belém and the new capital, Brasília, to the south.

Only in Belém and in Pucallpa is the river truly a part of the countries through which it flows. But did the people who scurried in the street know what a fantastic ocean of a river flowed at their feet? Beyond the port, the sun danced on the dark waters, shooting little stars of light onto the puffed sails of cutters heading upriver. The rivermen knew. We knew. In a few hours they would be surrounded by the jungle that has stirred hope and ambition for four centuries. And yet it sleeps. That green wasteland of hope and ambition,

HELEN AND FRANK SCHREIDER

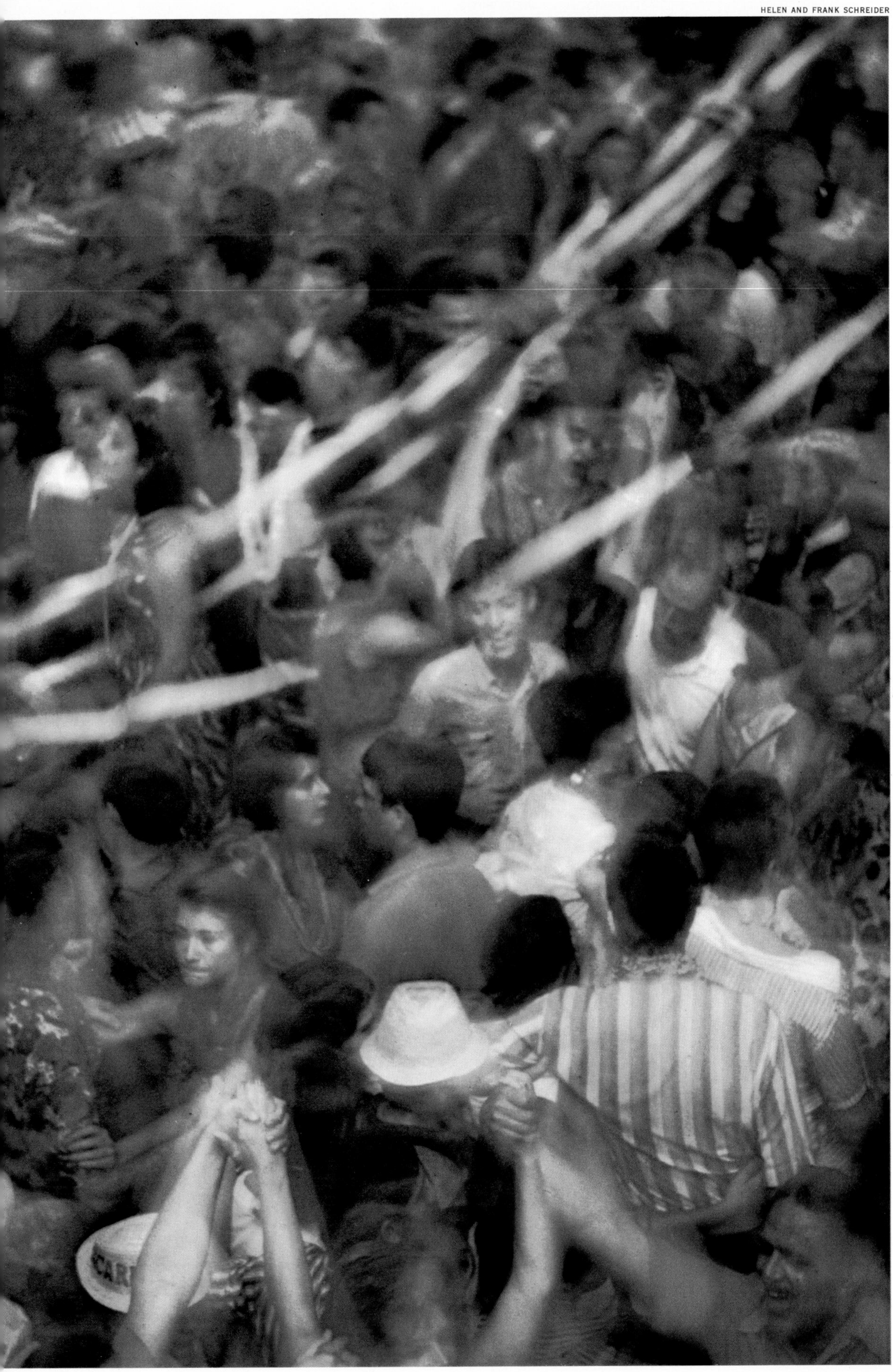

two hours from this living city, sleeps as it always has, as perhaps it always will.

But *would* it always sleep? While traveling the river I had said yes. Belém told me no. If this city could thrive and grow and prosper on the banks of the Amazon, so could Manaus, Iquitos, and dozens of other cities and towns.

My visit to ICOMI — Indústria e Comércio de Minérios S.A. — the huge manganese operation stretching inland from the north bank of the Amazon, also told me no. "What we can do, others can do," ICOMI's public relations manager, José Luis Freire, declared.

ICOMI has done a great deal. With 51 percent Brazilian and 49 percent U.S. ownership ICOMI has built hospitals, two model towns, 128 miles of railroad, a deepwater pier, and conveyor-belt loaders for the high-grade black ore so vital for steel production. After visiting well maintained homes, shops, and schools at the open-pit mine — 100 percent Brazilian managed and operated — I found my pessimism about the Amazon's future overlaid with enthusiasm. At dinner in the comfortable clubhouse, Senhor Freire explained some of the side effects of ICOMI's operations:

"We've proved that with preventive medicine the Amazon can be made livable. When you sprinkled salt on your steak just now, you took an antimalarial drug. The same drug is in every package of salt our employees buy from our company stores. We have malaria under control here. We have none of the endemic illnesses that plague other parts of the Amazon. Our health level is the highest in northern Brazil. Infant mortality, we believe, is the lowest in all of South America. Now we're working with people of the whole area, not just company employees. Other companies can do the same.

"But the Amazon needs settlers, not just adventurers who come to make a stake and move on. We need capital that will be reinvested, not taken back to the south of Brazil after a few years. Settlers, capital, health measures — with

Nursing infant dozes at his mother's breast aboard the steamer Amazonas, *heading downriver. During the trip, passengers berth in hammocks slung from posts between decks. Below, commuters share a floating school bus with youngsters bound for Belém.*

Gateway to the Amazon, Belém bulges like an equatorial Manhattan into Guajará Bay. The city—

founded by the Portuguese in 1615 — lies near the mouth of the Pará River 86 miles from the ocean.

these and a rational government program — the Amazon's riches can be tapped."

Whether Brazil, which controls the jaguar's share of the Amazon, can provide the capital and settlers remains to be seen. After centuries of neglect the Brazilian Government at last seems interested in its tremendous territory to the north. The Rondon Project — named for Gen. C. M. da Silva Rondon, who did so much to pacify the Indians half a century ago — has been started, rather like a short-term Brazilian Peace Corps.

To experience life in a part of their country most have only read about, college students from the south of Brazil spend their vacations working in Amazon villages. They wear T-shirts emblazoned with the slogan *Ocupamos ou Entregamos,* which in intent means "We must occupy the Amazon or we will lose it." In effect Brazilians are recognizing that man as well as nature abhors a vacuum. To whom does Brazil believe it might lose the Amazon? Not far from the airport at Macapá, where I landed to visit ICOMI, a star-shaped, 18th-century fort guards a mouth of the Amazon. The original stone tablet is gone now, but a copy explains that the fort had been built "to keep out the French gentleman, Dutch adventurer, and English buccaneer." Had there been such a thing when the fort was constructed, the words "American profiteer" might have been added.

To ultranationalistic Brazilians the Amazon is in danger. During our journey downriver we were told: that the United States plans to take over the area to resettle militant blacks; that the United Nations wants the Amazon to relieve population pressures in Asia; that 15,000 U. S. Marines were already en route to the Amazon. When the Hudson Institute, a New York "think tank," proposed damming the Amazon to make a huge inland sea that would provide access to remote jungle regions and generate unlimited hydroelectric power, propagandists claimed that the project was really a cover, that the United States wanted a protected nuclear submarine base.

Although few intelligent Brazilians believe these tales, the stories do illustrate the attitude of Brazilians toward foreign exploitation of the Amazon's riches. Brazil wants to — and should — develop the Amazon by herself. SUDAM has taken some giant steps in that direction just by establishing the tax-incentive program and coordinating plans. If carried beyond the planning stage — this is where most other schemes for the area have mired down — SUDAM's projects for electric power, communications, food processing, leather, cement, lumbering, plastics, and general industrial development could generate staggering changes along the Amazon.

But then the Amazon has always been staggering. As Helen, Balty, and I flew from Belém to the States it took 20 minutes at 600 miles an hour to cross the river, 200 miles wide at its mouth. Enough water flows from that mouth in one day to supply the city of New York for nine years.

The Amazon is a river — a land — of superlatives. It has the most trees, the longest snakes, the biggest rodents, and the greatest dreams. If past history is any indication, the task of turning even a small part of those dreams into reality will be staggering too.

One Greek myth gave the Amazon her name; another still echoes across her sepia waters. The Amazon, like the Land of the Lotus Eaters, long has lured man with her promises, and then lulled him to sleep.

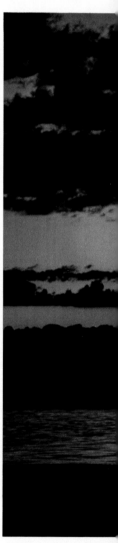

Fiery sunset over the Pará River outlines fishing boats anchored near Belém, where Helen and Frank Schreider concluded their 8¹/₂-month, adventure-filled odyssey down the Amazon. "Well, this is it. We made it," Frank said as they prepared to return home. And Helen replied softly, "No, we didn't make it. The river just let us go."

Index

Illustrations references appear in italics

Acknowledgements

The Special Publications Division is grateful to the people named or quoted in the text and to those listed here for their generous cooperation and assistance during the preparation of this book: William D. Field (insects), Richard C. Froeschner (insects), Melvin H. Jackson (boats), Ronald H. Pine (mammals), Velva E. Rudd (botany), Stanley H. Weitzman (fishes), George R. Zug (reptiles and amphibians), and Richard L. Zusi (birds), all Smithsonian Institution; C. Ralph Borthwick, Harriet Fields, Willard Kindberg, Harriet Kneeland, John N. Lindskoog, Wayne W. Snell, and Alva A. Wheeler, all Summer Institute of Linguistics; Ruy Alencar (Manaus), Instituto Cultural Brasil-Estados Unidos; E. Bradford Burns (Manaus), Department of History, University of California at Los Angeles; Guido Dolci (Atalaya); C. J. Hudig (rubber), Companhia Goodyear do Brasil; Georges E. Losson (rubber), International Bank for Reconstruction and Development; Roy E. Oltman (hydrology), U. S. Geological Survey.

Bibliography

The reader may wish to refer to the following books for related material:

GENERAL: Butland, Gilbert J., *Latin America: A Regional Geography,* 1966; Freyre, Gilberto, *New World in the Tropics,* 1959; Furneaux, Robin, *The Amazon: The Story of a Great River,* 1969; Gunther, John, *Inside South America,* 1967; Haskins, Caryl P., *The Amazon: The Life History of a Mighty River,* 1943; Huxley, Matthew, and Capa, Cornell, *Farewell to Eden,* 1964; James, Preston E., *Latin America,* 1969; Matthiessen, Peter, *The Cloud Forest,* 1961; Paddock, William and Paul, *Hungry Nations,* 1964; Rodman, Selden, *The Peru Traveler,* 1967; Schulthess, Emil, and Emil, Egli, *The Amazon,* 1962; Smithsonian Institution, *Handbook of South American Indians;* St. Clair, David, *The Mighty, Mighty Amazon,* 1968.

HISTORY: Bushnell, G.H.S., *Peru,* 1963; Cieza de León, Pedro de, *The Incas,* 1960; Freyre, Gilberto, *The Masters and the Slaves,* 1956; Hanson, Earl Parker, *South from the Spanish Main,* 1967; Innes, Hammond, *The Conquistadors,* 1969; Medina, José Toribio, *The Discovery of the Amazon,* 1934; Mason, J. Alden, *The Ancient Civilizations of Peru,* 1957; Millar, George R., *A Crossbowman's Story,* 1955; Monteiro, Mário Ypiranga, *Teatro Amazonas,* 1966; Prescott, William H., *History of the Conquest of Peru,* 1928.

EXPLORATION: Agassiz, Louis, *A Journey in Brazil,* 1909; Fleming, Peter, *Brazilian Adventure,* 1933; Herndon, Lt. William Lewis, *Exploration of the Valley of the Amazon, Part I,* 1854; Roosevelt, Theodore, *Through the Brazilian Wilderness,* 1919; Tomlinson, Henry Major, *The Sea and the Jungle,* 1920; Wallace, Alfred Russel, *Travels on the Amazon and Rio Negro,* 1889.

NATURAL HISTORY: Bates, Henry Walter, *The Naturalist on the River Amazons,* 1863; Cochran, Doris M., *Living Amphibians of the World,* 1961; Dorst, Jean, *South America and Central America,* 1967; Pope, Clifford H., *The Giant Snakes,* 1961; Sanderson, Ivan T., *Book of Great Jungles,* 1965; Walker, Ernest P., *Mammals of the World,* 1968.

For additional references, the reader may also wish to check the *National Geographic Index* for articles on Amazon Basin countries.

Composition for *Exploring the Amazon* by National Geographic's Phototypographic Division, Herman J.A.C. Arens, Director; John E. McConnell, Manager. Printed and bound by Fawcett-Haynes Printing Corp., Rockville, Md. Color separations by Beck Engraving Co., Philadelphia, Pa.; Graphic South, Inc., Charlotte, N.C.; The Lanman Co., Alexandria, Va; Lebanon Valley Offset, Inc., Cleona, Pa.; and Progressive Color Corp., Rockville, Md.

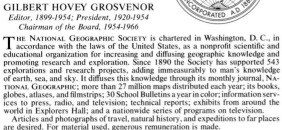